THE EOE DIET COOKBOOK

A Comprehensive Guide to Eating Well
and Improving Your Esophagus with
Delicious and Nutritious Recipes

WENDY S. LAINE

TABLE OF CONTENT

CHAPTER ONE

Understanding EoE and the Elimination Diet

Eosinophilic Esophagitis (EoE) is a chronic inflammatory condition of the esophagus, often triggered by specific foods. Traditional diagnostic methods like skin and blood tests are unreliable for identifying these triggers. The six-food elimination diet has emerged as a primary treatment option, excluding wheat, milk, soy, nuts, eggs, and seafood. Gradual reintroduction, confirmed through endoscopy, helps pinpoint trigger foods. This comprehensive guide sheds light on the importance of dietary management in mitigating EoE's impact on the esophagus.

Dietary choices play a pivotal role in alleviating inflammation and improving overall well-being for individuals with EoE. "The EOE Diet Cookbook" serves as a valuable resource, offering practical knowledge, EoE-compliant recipes, and insightful tips for creating a diverse and enjoyable meal plan. Recipes are thoughtfully crafted to align with the dietary restrictions associated with Eosinophilic Esophagitis, providing both symptom relief and an enhanced quality of life.

For those new to the EOE diet or seeking fresh inspiration, this cookbook provides a structured approach to meal planning and preparation. Delve into introductory chapters to gain a comprehensive understanding of EoE, its triggers, and the crucial role of dietary choices in managing symptoms. The recipes are clear, concise, and tailored to meet the unique needs of individuals with Eosinophilic Esophagitis.

Addressing the intricacies of Eosinophilic Esophagitis, the cookbook explores the elimination diet—a cornerstone in symptom alleviation. By systematically removing and reintroducing potential trigger foods, individuals can tailor their diets effectively, minimizing adverse effects. The step-up elimination approach, such as the 2–4–6 method, offers a less restrictive alternative, reducing unnecessary dietary restrictions and facilitating quicker identification of trigger foods.

Creating delicious and safe meals for EoE involves employing specific cooking techniques without compromising on flavor. From steaming and baking to grilling and sautéing with neutral oils, this cookbook guides readers on enhancing flavors while ensuring safety. The use of fresh herbs, mild spices, and allergen-free flour substitutes adds depth to EOE-friendly dishes. Collaboration with healthcare professionals remains key, ensuring a balanced and well-managed diet.

Living with Eosinophilic Esophagitis significantly impacts daily life. Symptoms, including difficulty swallowing, food impaction, reflux-like symptoms, and abdominal pain, lead to cautious eating habits. The chronic nature of EoE necessitates ongoing management and collaboration between individuals, healthcare providers, and dietitians. As understanding of EoE evolves, so do strategies for managing its impact on individuals' lives.

Creating an EOE-friendly kitchen involves selecting safe ingredients and understanding how to identify potential triggers. Lean proteins, non-citrus fruits, non-tomato-based sauces, whole grains, non-dairy milk alternatives, and fresh vegetables (non-trigger varieties) form the foundation of EOE-friendly ingredients. Keeping a food diary, implementing an elimination diet, reading food labels, and consulting with healthcare professionals are essential steps in this process.

The EOE elimination diet involves systematic removal of potential trigger foods, typically guided by healthcare professionals. Comprehensive allergy testing helps identify initial trigger foods, followed by an elimination phase where identified trigger foods are strictly avoided. Close monitoring of symptoms during this phase helps assess the diet's effectiveness. The reintroduction phase involves gradually reintroducing specific foods one at a time, observing for symptom recurrence, and developing a personalized, sustainable long-term diet plan.

Successful implementation of the elimination diet requires strict adherence to dietary restrictions, posing challenges in lifestyle adjustments and food choices. Collaboration with healthcare professionals is crucial for accurate identification of trigger foods and developing a suitable long-term diet plan. Patient education on reading food labels, identifying hidden allergens, and making informed food choices is integral.

Diet plays a fundamental role in managing Eosinophilic Esophagitis, influencing the frequency and intensity of symptoms. An EOE-friendly diet aims to alleviate symptoms such as difficulty swallowing, chest pain, and heartburn. While medical interventions may be part of the overall treatment plan, a carefully curated diet is often complementary and can enhance the effectiveness of other therapies.

Welcome to a culinary exploration that combines the science of EOE management with the art of creating flavorful and nourishing dishes. "The EOE Diet Cookbook" is not just a collection of recipes; it's your tool for empowerment and a celebration of the positive impact that thoughtful dietary choices can have on individuals facing the challenges of Eosinophilic Esophagitis.

Understanding EOE-Friendly Ingredients

Eosinophilic Esophagitis (EOE) demands a thoughtful and meticulous approach to dietary choices, focusing on ingredients that are less likely to trigger adverse reactions. Creating an EOE-friendly kitchen involves not only selecting safe ingredients but also understanding how to identify potential triggers. Here's a guide to understanding EOE-friendly ingredients and recognizing potential triggers:

Types of EOE-Friendly Ingredients

Lean Proteins

- Opt for lean proteins such as poultry, fish, and certain cuts of meat.

- **Plant-based proteins like beans, lentils, and tofu can be excellent alternatives.**

Non-Citrus Fruits

- Choose non-citrus fruits like apples, pears, and berries.
- These fruits are less likely to contribute to esophageal irritation.

Non-Tomato-Based Sauces

- Select sauces that do not contain tomatoes, as tomatoes can be a common trigger for EOE.
- Explore alternatives like olive oil-based dressings or pesto.

Whole Grains

- Opt for whole grains like rice, quinoa, and oats.
- These grains are often better tolerated than refined grains or wheat.

Non-Dairy Milk Alternatives

- Consider non-dairy milk alternatives such as almond, coconut, or oat milk.
- These options provide a substitute for individuals with lactose intolerance or dairy-related triggers.

Fresh Vegetables (Non-Trigger Varieties)

- Embrace vegetables that are less likely to cause irritation, such as carrots, cucumbers, and leafy greens.
- Steer clear of trigger vegetables like tomatoes, bell peppers, and onions.

Identifying Potential Triggers

Keep a Food Diary

- Maintain a detailed food diary to track what you eat and any associated symptoms.

- This can help identify patterns and potential trigger foods.

Elimination Diet

- Work with a healthcare professional to implement an elimination diet, removing common triggers and gradually reintroducing foods to pinpoint sensitivities.

Read Food Labels

- Scrutinize food labels for potential allergens and additives.
- Beware of hidden ingredients that may contribute to inflammation.

Be Mindful of Food Preparation

- Pay attention to cooking methods; grilled or baked foods may be better tolerated than fried or heavily processed options.
- Experiment with different cooking techniques to identify what works best.

Consult with Healthcare Professionals

- Collaborate with healthcare providers, including allergists and dietitians, to tailor dietary recommendations based on individual needs and sensitivities.

Understanding EOE-friendly ingredients involves a combination of selecting wisely, monitoring reactions, and maintaining open communication with healthcare professionals. With diligence and careful attention to individual responses, individuals with EOE can build a diverse and satisfying menu that aligns with their dietary needs.

Systematic Elimination

The elimination diet involves systematically removing potential trigger foods from the diet. This is typically done under the guidance of healthcare professionals, who help individuals identify specific allergens or irritants.

Comprehensive Allergy Testing

Before initiating the elimination phase, individuals may undergo comprehensive allergy testing, including skin prick tests or blood tests, to identify potential allergens. This informs the initial list of foods to be eliminated.

Elimination Phase

During this phase, individuals strictly avoid the identified trigger foods for a predetermined period, often several weeks to a few months. This allows the esophagus to heal and symptoms to subside.

Symptom Monitoring

Throughout the elimination phase, close monitoring of symptoms is essential. This helps assess the effectiveness of the diet in reducing eosinophilic inflammation in the esophagus.

Reintroduction Phase

Gradual Reintroduction: After the elimination phase, specific foods are gradually reintroduced one at a time. This is typically done in a structured manner under the guidance of a healthcare professional to pinpoint trigger foods.

Symptom Observation: During the reintroduction, individuals carefully observe for any recurrence of symptoms. If symptoms reappear, it indicates a potential trigger food, and its consumption is minimized or eliminated from the diet.

Individualized Diet Plan: Based on the reintroduction outcomes, a personalized and sustainable long-term diet plan is developed. This plan aims to maintain a nutritionally balanced diet while avoiding identified trigger foods.

Challenges and Considerations

Strict Adherence: Successful implementation of the elimination diet requires strict adherence to dietary restrictions, which may pose challenges in terms of lifestyle adjustments and food choices.

Professional Guidance: Collaboration with healthcare professionals, including dietitians and allergists, is crucial throughout the process to ensure accurate identification of trigger foods and the development of a suitable long-term diet plan.

Patient Education: Education on reading food labels, identifying hidden allergens, and making informed food choices is an integral part of the elimination diet process.

The EOE elimination diet is a dynamic and personalized journey that combines medical guidance with individual observations, aiming to enhance the quality of life for those managing Eosinophilic Esophagitis.

The Role of Diet in EOE Management

Fundamental Impact: Diet plays a fundamental role in the management of Eosinophilic Esophagitis (EOE), influencing both the frequency and intensity of symptoms. By strategically selecting foods that align with the elimination diet and avoiding triggers, individuals can actively mitigate inflammation in the esophagus.

Symptom Alleviation: An EOE-friendly diet aims to alleviate symptoms such as difficulty swallowing, chest pain, and heartburn. Understanding the relationship between specific foods and eosinophilic inflammation empowers individuals to take control of their symptoms through dietary choices.

Complementary to Medical Interventions: While medical interventions may be part of the overall treatment plan, a carefully curated diet is often complementary and can enhance the effectiveness of other therapies. Dietary management addresses the root cause of EOE symptoms by minimizing exposure to triggering substances.

Navigating the EOE Diet with This Cookbook

Comprehensive Guidance: This cookbook serves as a comprehensive guide for individuals navigating the complexities of the EOE diet. It provides practical insights, EOE-compliant recipes, and essential tips to support readers in creating a diverse and enjoyable meal plan that aligns with their dietary restrictions.

Structured Approach: Organized by meal type, the cookbook offers a structured approach to meal planning, making it accessible for both newcomers to the EOE diet and those seeking fresh inspiration. The recipes are crafted to be flavorful, diverse, and nutritionally balanced, ensuring a positive culinary experience.

Empowering Choices: By offering a range of recipes and educational content, this cookbook aims to empower individuals to make informed choices about their dietary habits. It encourages readers to explore the positive impact that thoughtful and EOE-compliant meals can have on their overall well-being.

Utilizing the Elimination Diet: Incorporating insights from the elimination diet, the cookbook guides individuals through the process of identifying trigger foods, implementing the elimination phase, and gradually reintroducing foods. It supports readers in customizing their diet based on personal observations and professional guidance.

Embrace the journey of managing Eosinophilic Esophagitis through dietary choices with confidence and culinary creativity. This cookbook is designed to be a valuable companion, providing not only recipes but also a holistic understanding of the pivotal role that diet plays in EOE management.

Oesinophilic esophagitis, or EoE, is a disorder in which the lining of the esophagus becomes inflamed and difficult to swallow due to an accumulation of white blood cells called eosinophils. Certain meals that produce an allergic reaction in the esophagus can set off an episode of eosinophilia (EoE). Some persons with EoE adopt an elimination diet, which eliminates the most frequent allergens from their diet and then reintroduces them one at a time to determine which ones trigger symptoms, in order to identify and avoid these items.

Elimination diets come in various forms for those with eating disorders, including the four food elimination diet (4FED) and the six food elimination diet (SFED). Whereas the 4FED also prohibits cow's milk, eggs, peanuts, tree nuts, soy, and wheat, the SFED does not. The reason these foods were selected is that they are the most likely to induce EoE in both adults and children. Before beginning an elimination diet, it's crucial to speak with a doctor and a nutritionist because some people may have additional food triggers that are not covered by these plans.

It might be difficult to stick to an elimination diet for EoE because it calls for avoiding a lot of common foods and substances, even in tiny amounts. To preserve a healthy and well-balanced diet, several alternatives to the foods that have been omitted can be employed. The following foods can be used in place of the SFED and 4FED:

Cow's milk: Found in a variety of dairy products, including cheese, yogurt, ice cream, butter, and cream, cow's milk is one of the most frequent causes of EoE. Fortified rice milk, hemp milk, coconut milk, and flax milk are a few alternatives to cow's milk. You can use these plant-based milks for baking, cooking, blending, and sipping. But, as they could differ from cow's milk in terms of flavor, texture, and nutritional content, it's crucial to study the labels and select the options that best fit your requirements. Keep in mind that since almond and cashew milks are manufactured from tree nuts, which are also excluded from the SFED, they cannot be used in place of cow's milk.

- Eggs: Found in a lot of baked goods, pastries, pancakes, waffles, mayonnaise, and sauces, eggs are another prominent cause of egg allergy syndrome. Applesauce, mashed bananas, chia seeds, flax seeds, and commercial egg replacers are a few egg substitutes. While these egg replacements are useful for binding, moistening, and leavening baked foods, they might not be the best choice for recipes like omelets, quiches, and custards that call for eggs as the primary component. A flax or chia egg is made by combining one tablespoon of ground flax or chia seeds with three tablespoons of water, then letting it sit until it gels, about fifteen minutes. You may use this in most recipes that call for eggs because it equals one egg. Tree nuts and peanuts: Found in a variety of baked products, cereals, granola bars, snacks, and nut butters, these two major EoE triggers can also cause allergic reactions. Sesame, hemp, sunflower, and pumpkin seeds are a few types of seeds that can be used in place of peanuts and tree nuts. You can consume these seeds raw, roast them, or process them to make seed butters like tahini or sunflower seed butter. They can also be used to flavor and crisp stir-fries, salads, and porridge. Before including seeds in your diet, consult your doctor as some individuals with EoE may also be allergic to them.

- Soy: Another popular cause of egg allergy syndrome is soy, which is present in a wide range of goods including tempeh, tofu, soy milk, soy sauce, soybean oil, and soy lecithin. Rice, quinoa, beans, lentils, and chickpeas are a few alternatives to soy. These foods can be used to produce rice bowls, falafel, hummus, and bean burgers, among other recipes, and can supply the protein, fiber, and other nutrients that soy can deliver. Coconut aminos, a soy-free sauce derived from coconut sap, can be used in place of soy sauce. You can use coconut oil, canola oil, or olive oil in place of soybean oil. Sunflower lecithin, an emulsifier free of soy, can be used in place of soy lecithin, which is used in some baked products and chocolates.

- Wheat: Among adult onset EoE triggers, wheat is present in a wide variety of foods, including bread, pasta, noodles, crackers, cookies, cakes, and cereals. Gluten-free grains including rice, quinoa, buckwheat, millet, and oats can be used in place of wheat. You can use these grains to make oatmeal, salads, soups, crackers, cookies, cakes, and gluten-free bread, pasta, and noodles. However, it's crucial to carefully read the labels and select the gluten-free goods that are suitable for you because some may include other allergies like eggs, milk, or soy. Additionally, because barley, rye, and oats may have proteins identical to those found in wheat, which can induce EoE, some individuals with the condition may need to avoid all grains that contain gluten. Before including these grains into your diet, talk about this with your physician and dietician.

You can identify and stay away from the items causing your symptoms by adhering to an elimination diet for EoE, but it can also be restrictive and challenging to follow. Thus, it's critical that you obtain medical advice and assistance from a nutritionist and doctor. They can assist you in creating a safe, well-balanced diet that satisfies your dietary requirements and tastes.

They can also assist you in keeping an eye on your symptoms and provide guidance on a methodical and controlled reintroduction of the items you have eliminated. You can enhance your quality of life and enjoy eating without discomfort by adhering to an elimination diet for ear, nose, and throat.

FOOD SUBSTITUTE

Wheat Substitutes in Recipes:

In recipes calling for wheat flour, you can substitute with these flour sources:

- Quinoa Flour
- Buckwheat Flour
- Gluten-Free Oats
- Brown Rice Flour

- Millet Flour

Milk Substitutes:

For those looking to avoid cow's milk while maintaining similar nutritional value, consider these substitutes:

- Fortified Rice Milk

- Fortified Hemp Milk

- Flax Milk

Egg Replacements in Cooking:

Replacing eggs can be challenging due to their various roles in food preparation. Here are some alternatives:

Flaxseed Flour Substitute for 1 Egg – Great for Binding

1 tablespoon Flaxseed Flour

3 tablespoons Water (stir until egg-like consistency)

Chia Seed Substitute for 1 Egg – Great for Leavening

1 tablespoon Chia Seed

1/3 cup Water (stir and let sit for 15 minutes)

Agar Agar Substitute for 1 Egg – Great for Binding

1 tablespoon Agar Agar

3 tablespoons Water

Ripe Bananas Substitute for 1 Egg – Great for Moisture

1/2 cup Mashed Bananas

Applesauce Substitute for 1 Egg – Great for Moisture

1/4 cup Applesauce (unsweetened)

Mashed Potatoes Substitute for 1 Egg – Great for Binding

2 tablespoons Mashed Potatoes (White or Sweet)

Nut and Seafood Substitutes:

Nuts: Peanuts and tree nuts are often used for taste and texture in recipes. While they can typically be skipped, you might try replacing them with rice cereal or a gluten-free whole grain if desired.

Seafood

Fish and shellfish are rich sources of protein and Omega-3 fatty acids. While it's difficult to find exact replacements, you can opt for low-fat meats like poultry for protein and increase consumption of flaxseed and canola oil for Omega-3 fatty acids.

Additional Ingredients:

Chickpeas

Coconut Milk

Clive Juice (possibly a typo, could be clarified)

Plum Vinegar

CHAPTER TWO

Breakfast Delights

Chia Pudding Parfait

⏱ 10 minutes 👨‍🍳 Refrigerate for at least 4 hours or overnight

Ingredients

- 1/4 cup chia seeds

- 1 cup unsweetened almond milk

- 1 tablespoon maple syrup (optional, depending on sweetness preference)

- 1/2 teaspoon vanilla extract

- Mixed berries (strawberries, blueberries, raspberries) for layering

- Shredded coconut for garnish

Instructions

I. In a bowl, combine chia seeds, almond milk, maple syrup (if using), and vanilla extract.

II. Whisk the mixture thoroughly to ensure that the chia seeds are evenly distributed.

III. Let it sit for a couple of minutes, then whisk again to avoid clumping.

IV. Cover the bowl and refrigerate for at least 4 hours or overnight to allow the chia seeds to absorb the liquid and form a pudding-like consistency.

V. Once the chia pudding is set, take it out of the refrigerator.

VI. In serving glasses or bowls, layer the chia pudding with mixed berries.

VII. Repeat the layers until the glass is filled, ending with a layer of berries on top.

VIII. Sprinkle shredded coconut on top for a delightful garnish.

IX. Serve chilled and enjoy your delicious Chia Pudding Parfait!

Estimated Nutritional Value (per serving)

Calories: 250, Protein: 6g, Fat: 12g, Carbohydrates: 30g, Fiber: 15g, Sugar: 8g

Tips:

Customize with your favorite berries or fruits. Add a dollop of dairy-free yogurt for extra creaminess. Sprinkle chopped nuts, such as almonds or walnuts, for added crunch. Adjust sweetness by adding more or less maple syrup. Experiment with different fruit combinations for variety. Make it the night before for a quick and nutritious breakfast option.

Banana-Oat Pancakes

 Prep Time: 10 minutes   Cook Time: 10 minutes

Ingredients

- 1 cup gluten-free oats

- 1 ripe banana

- 1 cup unsweetened almond milk

- 1 teaspoon baking powder

- 1/2 teaspoon vanilla extract

- Pinch of salt

- Coconut oil for cooking

Instructions

I. In a blender, combine oats, ripe banana, almond milk, baking powder, vanilla extract, and a pinch of salt.

II. Blend until you have a smooth pancake batter.

III. Heat a non-stick skillet or griddle over medium heat.

IV. Lightly grease the surface with coconut oil.

V. Pour 1/4 cup of batter onto the hot skillet for each pancake.

VI. Cook until bubbles form on the surface, then flip and cook the other side until golden brown.

VII. Stack the pancakes on a plate.

VIII. Top with sliced bananas, a drizzle of maple syrup, or a sprinkle of shredded coconut.

IX. Serve warm and enjoy your delicious Banana-Oat Pancakes!

Estimated Nutritional Value (per serving)

Calories: 250, Protein: 5g, Fat: 8g, Carbohydrates: 40g, Fiber: 5g, Sugar: 8g

Tips:

Ensure the skillet is hot before pouring the batter to achieve fluffy pancakes.

Make a larger batch and freeze extras for a quick breakfast option during the week.

Experiment with different gluten-free flours for variety.

Sweet Potato Hash Browns

 Prep Time: 15 minutes Cook Time: 20 minutes

Ingredients

- 2 medium-sized sweet potatoes, peeled and grated

- 1 small onion, finely chopped

- 2 tablespoons arrowroot powder or cornstarch

- 1 teaspoon paprika

- 1/2 teaspoon garlic powder

- Salt and pepper to taste

- 2-3 tablespoons coconut oil for cooking

Instructions

I. Peel and grate the sweet potatoes. Place them in a clean kitchen towel and squeeze out excess moisture.

II. In a mixing bowl, combine grated sweet potatoes, chopped onion, arrowroot powder (or cornstarch), paprika, garlic powder, salt, and pepper. Mix well until evenly combined.

III. Take a portion of the mixture and shape it into a patty, pressing it firmly together.

IV. Heat coconut oil in a skillet over medium heat.

V. Place the shaped sweet potato patties in the skillet and cook for about 4-5 minutes on each side, or until they are golden brown and crispy.

VI. Remove from the skillet and place on a plate lined with a paper towel to absorb any excess oil.

VII. Serve the Sweet Potato Hash Browns warm as a delicious and wholesome side dish.

Estimated Nutritional Value (per serving)

Calories: 180, Protein: 2g, Fat: 8g, Carbohydrates: 25g, Fiber: 4g, Sugar: 5g

Tips:

Ensure the grated sweet potatoes are well-drained to achieve crispiness. Adjust the seasoning according to your taste preferences. For an extra kick, add a pinch of cayenne pepper or chili flakes to the mixture.

Avocado and Tomato Breakfast Wrap

 Prep Time: 10 minutes   Cook Time: 5 minutes

Ingredients

- 1 large avocado, sliced

- 1 medium-sized tomato, sliced

- 2 gluten-free brown rice tortillas

- 1 tablespoon olive oil

- Salt and pepper to taste

- Fresh cilantro leaves for garnish (optional)

Instructions

I. Slice the avocado and tomato.

II. In a dry skillet over medium heat, warm the brown

rice tortillas for about 20-30 seconds on each side.

III. Lay out the warm tortillas on a flat surface.

IV. Place slices of avocado and tomato in the center of each tortilla.

V. Drizzle olive oil over the avocado and tomato slices.

VI. Sprinkle with salt and pepper to taste.

VII. Fold in the sides of the tortilla and then roll it up tightly to create the wrap.

VIII. Place the wraps seam-side down on a plate.

IX. Garnish with fresh cilantro leaves for an extra burst of flavor.

X. Serve immediately and enjoy your Avocado and Tomato Breakfast Wrap!

Estimated Nutritional Value (per serving)

Calories: 300, Protein: 5g, Fat: 20g, Carbohydrates: 30g, Fiber: 8g, Sugar: 2g

Tips:

Choose ripe avocados for creaminess.

Warm tortillas just enough to make them pliable.

Experiment with different gluten-free tortilla varieties for variety.

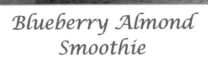

Blueberry Almond Smoothie

 Prep Time: 5 minutes   Cook Time: 0 minutes

Ingredients

- 1 cup frozen blueberries
- 1 ripe banana
- 1 cup unsweetened almond milk
- 2 tablespoons almond butter
- 1 tablespoon chia seeds
- Ice cubes (optional)

Instructions

I.   Peel the ripe banana.

In a blender, combine frozen blueberries, peeled banana, almond milk, almond butter, and chia seeds.

II.   If you prefer a colder smoothie, you can add a
        handful of ice cubes.

III.   Blend on high speed until the mixture is smooth
        and creamy.

IV.   Enjoy your refreshing Blueberry Almond Smoothie
        immediately!

Estimated Nutritional Value (per serving)

Calories: 300, Protein: 7g, Fat: 15g, Carbohydrates: 35g, Fiber: 9g, Sugar: 15g

Tips

Use frozen blueberries for a colder and thicker consistency.

Adjust the thickness by adding more or less almond milk.

Customize by incorporating other dairy-free milk alternatives such as coconut or oat milk.

Spinach and Mushroom Frittata

 Prep Time: 15 minutes   Cook Time: 20 minutes

Ingredients

- 1 cup fresh spinach, chopped
- 1 cup mushrooms, sliced
- 1 small onion, finely chopped
- 1 tablespoon olive oil
- Flaxseeds
- 1/4 cup unsweetened almond milk
- Salt and pepper to taste
- 1/2 teaspoon garlic powder
- 1/2 cup dairy-free cheese, shredded (optional)
- Fresh herbs (parsley, thyme) for garnish

Instructions

I.   Preheat the oven to 375°F (190°C).

II.   In an oven-safe skillet, heat olive oil over medium heat.

III. Add chopped onion and sliced mushrooms, sauté until softened, about 5 minutes.

IV.   Add chopped spinach and continue cooking until wilted.

V.   In a bowl, whisk together flaxseeds, almond milk, salt, pepper, and garlic powder.

VI.   Pour the egg mixture into the skillet over the sautéed vegetables.

VII. Gently stir to combine the ingredients evenly.

VIII. Sprinkle dairy-free cheese on top if using.

IX.   Let the frittata cook on the stovetop for 3-4 minutes, or until the edges start to set.

X.   Transfer the skillet to the preheated oven and bake for 15-20 minutes, or until the center is set and the top is golden brown.

XI.   Garnish with fresh herbs.

XII.   Slice the frittata into wedges and serve warm.

Estimated Nutritional Value (per serving)

Calories: 180, Protein: 15g, Fat: 12g, Carbohydrates: 5g, Fiber: 2g, Sugar: 2g

Tips

Feel free to add other vegetables like bell peppers or tomatoes.

Use a well-seasoned cast-iron skillet for optimal results.

Customize with your favorite herbs or spices.

Rice Porridge with Cinnamon Apples

 Prep Time: 10 minutes   Cook Time: 25 minutes

Ingredients

- 1 cup white rice (short-grain or jasmine)

- 4 cups unsweetened almond milk

- 2 tablespoons maple syrup (optional)

- 1 teaspoon vanilla extract

- 1/2 teaspoon ground cinnamon

- Pinch of salt

- 2 medium-sized apples, peeled, cored, and diced

- 1 tablespoon coconut oil

- Chopped nuts (almonds, walnuts) for garnish

- Additional cinnamon for sprinkling

Instructions

I.   Rinse the rice under cold water.

II.   In a medium-sized pot, combine rice, almond milk, maple syrup (if using), vanilla extract, ground cinnamon, and a pinch of salt.

III.   Bring the mixture to a boil, then reduce heat to low, cover, and simmer for 20-25 minutes, or until the rice is cooked and the porridge thickens. Stir occasionally.

IV.   While the rice is cooking, heat coconut oil in a skillet over medium heat.

V.   Add diced apples and sauté until they are tender, about 5-7 minutes.

VI.   Sprinkle with a little cinnamon and toss to coat the apples evenly.

VII.   Once the rice porridge is ready, spoon it into bowls.

VIII.   Top the rice porridge with the sautéed cinnamon

apples.

IX.   Sprinkle chopped nuts over the apples for added

crunch.

X.   Serve warm, optionally drizzling a bit more maple

syrup on top.

Estimated Nutritional Value (per serving)

Calories: 300, Protein: 5g, Fat: 8g, Carbohydrates: 55g, Fiber: 5g, Sugar: 15g

Tips

Adjust sweetness with more or less maple syrup, based on preference.

Experiment with different varieties of apples for diverse flavors.

For a creamier texture, stir in a spoonful of dairy-free yogurt.

Zucchini and Tomato Breakfast Casserole

Zucchini and Tomato Breakfast Casserole

 Prep Time: 15 minutes   Cook Time: 35 minutes

Ingredients

- 2 medium-sized zucchini, thinly sliced

- 1 cup cherry tomatoes, halved

- 1 small onion, finely chopped

- 2 cloves garlic, minced

- 1 tablespoon olive oil

- 1/4 cup unsweetened almond milk

- Salt and pepper to taste

- 1 teaspoon dried oregano

- 1 cup dairy-free cheese, shredded (optional)

- Fresh basil leaves for garnish

Instructions

I. Preheat the oven to 375°F (190°C).

II. In a skillet, heat olive oil over medium heat.

III. Add chopped onion and minced garlic, sauté until softened.

IV. Add sliced zucchini and cook until slightly tender.

V. Stir in cherry tomatoes and cook for an additional 2-3 minutes. Remove from heat.

VI. In a greased baking dish, spread the sautéed vegetables evenly.

VII. Pour the mixture over the vegetables.

VIII. If using, sprinkle dairy-free cheese on top.

IX. Bake in the preheated oven for 30-35 minutes or until the eggs are set and the top is golden brown.

X. Garnish with fresh basil leaves.

XI. Allow the casserole to cool slightly before slicing and serving.

Estimated Nutritional Value (per serving)

Calories: 220, Protein: 14g, Fat: 15g, Carbohydrates: 8g, Fiber: 2g, Sugar: 4g

Tips

Feel free to add other vegetables such as bell peppers or spinach.

Use a well-seasoned cast-iron skillet or a baking dish.

Customize with your favorite herbs or spices.

Quinoa Banana Muffins

 Prep Time: 15 minutes   Cook Time: 20 minutes

Ingredients

- 1 cup cooked quinoa, cooled

- 2 ripe bananas, mashed

- 1/4 cup coconut oil, melted

- 1/4 cup maple syrup or agave nectar

- 1 teaspoon vanilla extract

- 1 cup gluten-free all-purpose flour

- 1 teaspoon baking powder

- 1/2 teaspoon baking soda

- 1/2 teaspoon ground cinnamon

- Pinch of salt

- 1/2 cup dairy-free milk (almond, coconut, or soy)

- 1/4 cup sunflower seeds, optional

Instructions

I. Preheat the oven to 350°F (175°C).

II. Line a muffin tin with paper liners or grease with a bit of coconut oil.

III. In a bowl, combine mashed bananas, melted coconut oil, maple syrup (or agave nectar), and vanilla extract. Mix well.

IV. In a separate bowl, whisk together gluten-free flour, baking powder, baking soda, ground cinnamon, and a pinch of salt.

V. Add the cooked quinoa to the wet ingredients and mix.

VI. Gradually add the dry ingredients to the wet ingredients, mixing until just combined.

VII. Pour in the dairy-free milk and stir until the batter is well combined.

VIII. If using, fold in the sunflower seeds into the batter.

IX. Spoon the batter into the muffin cups, filling each about two-thirds full.

X. Bake in the preheated oven for 18-20 minutes or until a toothpick inserted into the center of a muffin comes out clean.

XI. Allow the muffins to cool in the tin for 5 minutes, then transfer them to a wire rack to cool completely.

Estimated Nutritional Value (per muffin)

Calories: 180, Protein: 3g, Fat: 8g, Carbohydrates: 25g, Fiber: 3g,Sugar: 8g

Tips

Ensure the quinoa is cooked and cooled before adding it to the batter.

Experiment with different gluten-free flour blends. Customize by adding dried fruits or chocolate chips if desired.

Pineapple Coconut Smoothie

 Prep Time: 5 minutes   Cook Time: 0 minutes

Ingredients

- 1 cup frozen pineapple chunks

- 1/2 cup coconut milk (canned, full-fat)

- 1/2 cup unsweetened coconut water

- 1/2 banana, frozen

- 1 tablespoon shredded coconut (optional, for garnish)

- Ice cubes (optional)

Instructions

I.   In a blender, combine frozen pineapple chunks, coconut milk, coconut water, and the frozen banana.

II.   Blend on high speed until the mixture is smooth and creamy.

III.   If you prefer a thicker smoothie, add a handful of ice cubes and blend again until smooth.

IV.   Pour the smoothie into a glass.

V.   Garnish with shredded coconut on top for added texture.

VI.   Enjoy your refreshing Pineapple Coconut Smoothie immediately!

Estimated Nutritional Value (per serving)

Calories: 250, Protein: 2g, Fat: 15g, Carbohydrates: 30g, Fiber: 5g, Sugar: 18g

Tips

Use frozen pineapple for a chilled and thicker consistency.

Adjust sweetness by adding more or less banana.

Experiment with different dairy-free milk alternatives for variety.

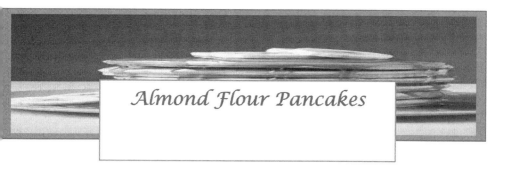

Almond Flour Pancakes

 Prep Time: 10 minutes   Cook Time: 10 minutes

Ingredients

- 1 cup almond flour

- 2 tablespoons coconut flour

- 1 teaspoon baking powder

- Pinch of salt

- 2 large bananas

- 1/2 cup unsweetened almond milk

- 1 tablespoon maple syrup (optional)

- 1 teaspoon vanilla extract

- Coconut oil for cooking

Instructions

I.   In a bowl, whisk together almond flour, coconut flour, baking powder, and a pinch of salt.

II.   In a separate bowl, mash the bananas and then add almond milk, maple syrup (if using), and vanilla extract. Mix well.

III.   Pour the wet ingredients into the dry ingredients and stir until just combined. Let the batter rest for a few minutes to thicken.

IV.   Heat a non-stick skillet or griddle over medium heat. Add a small amount of coconut oil to coat the surface.

V.   Spoon 1/4 cup of batter onto the skillet for each pancake.

VI.   Cook until bubbles form on the surface, then flip and cook the other side until golden brown.

VII.   Stack the pancakes on a plate.

VIII.   Serve warm and enjoy your delicious Almond Flour

Pancakes!

Estimated Nutritional Value (per serving)

Calories: 180, Protein: 7g, Fat: 15g, Carbohydrates: 6g, Fiber: 3g, Sugar: 2g

Tips

Ensure the skillet is hot before pouring the batter to achieve fluffy pancakes.

Adjust sweetness by adding more or less maple syrup.

Experiment with different extracts such as almond or lemon for unique flavors.

Mango and Coconut Chia Pudding

 Prep Time: 10 minutes   Chilling Time: 4hours

Ingredients

- 1/4 cup chia seeds

- 1 cup coconut milk (canned, full-fat)

- 1 tablespoon maple syrup or agave nectar

- 1/2 teaspoon vanilla extract

- 1 ripe mango, diced

- Shredded coconut for garnish

Instructions

I.   In a bowl, combine chia seeds, coconut milk, maple syrup (or agave nectar), and vanilla extract.

II.   Whisk the mixture thoroughly to ensure chia seeds are evenly distributed.

III.   Let it sit for a couple of minutes, then whisk again to avoid clumping.

IV.   Cover the bowl and refrigerate for at least 4 hours or overnight, allowing the chia seeds to absorb the liquid and form a pudding-like consistency.

V.   After the chia pudding base has set, spoon a layer of diced mango on top.

VI.   Sprinkle shredded coconut on top for a delightful garnish.

VII.   If desired, return the pudding to the refrigerator for an additional 30 minutes to chill the mango layer.

VIII.   Serve chilled and enjoy your Mango and Coconut Chia Pudding!

Estimated Nutritional Value (per serving)

Calories: 250, Protein: 4g, Fat: 15g, Carbohydrates: 25g, Fiber: 8g, Sugar: 15g

Tips

Adjust sweetness by adding more or less maple syrup.

Experiment with different tropical fruits for variety.

Make it the night before for a quick and nutritious breakfast or dessert option.

Hashed Brown Potatoes with Peppers

Hashed Brown Potatoes with Peppers

 Prep Time: 15 minutes   Cook Time: 20 minutes

Ingredients

- 4 medium-sized russet potatoes, peeled and grated

- 1 bell pepper (any color), diced

- 1 small onion, finely chopped

- 2 tablespoons olive oil

- 1 teaspoon paprika

- Salt and pepper to taste

- Fresh parsley for garnish (optional)

Instructions

I. Peel the potatoes and grate them using a box grater. Squeeze out any excess moisture using a clean kitchen towel.

II. In a large skillet, heat olive oil over medium heat.

III. Add finely chopped onion and diced bell pepper. Sauté until the vegetables are softened.

IV. Add the grated potatoes to the skillet, spreading them out evenly.

V. Sprinkle paprika, salt, and pepper over the potatoes. Mix well.

VI. Allow the potatoes to cook without stirring for a few minutes until the bottom

VII. Flip and Cook:

VIII. Flip portions of the potatoes and cook the other side until the entire hash is golden brown and crispy.

IX. Garnish with fresh parsley if desired.

X.   Serve the Hashed Brown Potatoes with Peppers warm.

Estimated Nutritional Value (per serving)

Calories: 200, Protein: 3g, Fat: 8g, Carbohydrates: 30g, Fiber: 4g, Sugar: 2g

Tips

Ensure the skillet is hot before adding the grated potatoes to achieve crispiness.

Experiment with different types of bell peppers for added color.

Customize with additional herbs or spices, such as garlic powder or cayenne pepper.

Raspberry Coconut Overnight Oats

 Prep Time: 10 minutes   Chilling Time: Overnight

Ingredients

- 1/2 cup rolled oats

- 1/2 cup coconut milk (canned, full-fat)

- 1/2 cup dairy-free yogurt (coconut or almond)

- 1/4 cup fresh raspberries

- 1 tablespoon chia seeds

- 1 tablespoon shredded coconut

- 1 tablespoon maple syrup or agave nectar

- 1/2 teaspoon vanilla extract

Instructions

I. In a jar or container with a lid, combine rolled oats, coconut milk, dairy-free yogurt, chia seeds, shredded coconut, maple syrup (or agave nectar), and vanilla extract.

II. Stir the ingredients thoroughly until well combined.

III. Gently fold in the fresh raspberries.

IV. Cover the jar or container with a lid and refrigerate overnight or for at least 4 hours, allowing the oats to absorb the liquid and soften.

V. Before serving, give the mixture a good stir to ensure an even consistency.

VI. Serve the Raspberry Coconut Overnight Oats cold.

Estimated Nutritional Value (per serving)

Calories: 350, Protein: 7g, Fat: 20g, Carbohydrates: 35g, Fiber: 8g, Sugar: 10g

Tips

Experiment with other berries or a mix of berries for variety.

Adjust sweetness by adding more or less maple syrup.

Prepare multiple jars for a quick and convenient grab-and-go breakfast throughout the week.

Acorn Squash Breakfast Bowl

Ingredients

- 1 acorn squash, halved and seeds removed

- 2 tablespoons coconut oil, melted

- 2 tablespoons maple syrup

- 1 teaspoon cinnamon

- 1/2 cup granola (choose a gluten-free variety)

- 1/4 cup chopped nuts (walnuts, pecans, or almonds)

- 1/4 cup dried fruits (cranberries, raisins, or chopped apricots)

- 1 tablespoon chia seeds

- Dairy-free yogurt for serving

Instructions

I.   Preheat the oven to 400°F (200°C).

II.   Place the acorn squash halves on a baking sheet, cut side up.

III. In a small bowl, mix the melted coconut oil, maple syrup, and cinnamon. Brush the mixture over the cut sides of the acorn squash.

IV.   Bake in the preheated oven for about 30 minutes or until the squash is tender and can be easily pierced with a fork.

V.   In a separate bowl, mix together granola, chopped nuts, dried fruits, and chia seeds.

VI.   Once the acorn squash is cooked, fill each half with the granola mixture.

VII. Top with a dollop of dairy-free yogurt.

VIII. Serve warm and enjoy your nutritious Acorn Squash Breakfast Bowl!

Estimated Nutritional Value (per serving)

Calories: 350, Protein: 5g, Fat: 18g, Carbohydrates: 45g, Fiber: 8g, Sugar: 18g

Tips

Ensure the acorn squash is fully cooked to maximize its sweetness and tenderness.

Experiment with different granola flavors for variety.

Feel free to add a dash of vanilla extract to the coconut oil and maple syrup mixture for extra flavor.

CHAPTER THREE

Lunch and dinner

Cauliflower Rice Stir-Fry

 Prep Time: 15 minutes   Cook Time: 15 minutes

Ingredients

- 1 medium-sized cauliflower, grated or processed into rice-like texture

- 2 tablespoons coconut oil or sesame oil

- 1 cup broccoli florets

- 1 medium carrot, julienned

- 1 bell pepper, thinly sliced

- 1 cup snap peas, trimmed

- 3 cloves garlic, minced

- 1 tablespoon fresh ginger, grated

- 1/4 cup low-sodium soy sauce or tamari (gluten-free option)

- 2 tablespoons rice vinegar

- 1 tablespoon sesame seeds (optional)

- Green onions, sliced, for garnish

- Salt and pepper to taste

Instructions

I. Grate the cauliflower using a box grater or process it in a food processor until it resembles rice. Set aside.

II. In a large skillet or wok, heat coconut oil over medium-high heat.

III. Add minced garlic and grated ginger, sautéing for about 30 seconds until fragrant.

IV.	Add broccoli, julienned carrot, sliced bell pepper, and snap peas to the skillet. Stir-fry for 3-5 minutes until the vegetables are slightly tender but still crisp.

V.	Push the vegetables to the side of the skillet and add the cauliflower rice. Cook for an additional 3-5 minutes, stirring occasionally, until the cauliflower rice is cooked through.

VI.	In a small bowl, mix soy sauce (or tamari) and rice vinegar. Pour the sauce over the cauliflower rice and vegetables. Toss everything together until well combined.

VII.	Season with salt and pepper to taste. Adjust the seasoning and soy sauce as needed.

VIII.	Garnish with sesame seeds (if using) and sliced green onions.

IX.   Serve the Cauliflower Rice Stir-Fry warm as a delicious and low-carb alternative to traditional stir-fried rice.

Estimated Nutritional Value (per serving)

Calories: 150, Protein: 5g, Fat: 8g, Carbohydrates: 18g, Fiber: 7g, Sugar: 7g

Tips

Ensure the cauliflower rice is well-drained to avoid excess moisture in the stir-fry.

Customize with additional vegetables such as mushrooms, water chestnuts, or baby corn.

Experiment with different low-carb sauces or add a dash of Sriracha for some heat.

Spaghetti Squash Primavera

 Prep Time: 15 minutes　　 **Cook Time: 40 minutes**

Ingredients

- 1 medium-sized spaghetti squash

- 2 tablespoons olive oil

- 1 small red onion, thinly sliced

- 2 cloves garlic, minced

- 1 bell pepper, thinly sliced

- 1 medium-sized zucchini, julienned

- 1 medium-sized carrot, julienned

- 1 cup cherry tomatoes, halved

- 1 cup broccoli florets

- 1/4 cup fresh basil, chopped

- Salt and pepper to taste

- 1/4 cup grated vegan Parmesan cheese (optional)

- Crushed red pepper flakes (optional, for added heat)

Instructions

I. Preheat the oven to 375°F (190°C).

II. Cut the spaghetti squash in half lengthwise. Scoop out the seeds.

III. Drizzle the cut sides with olive oil and season with salt and pepper.

IV. Place the squash, cut side down, on a baking sheet.

V. Bake in the preheated oven for 35-40 minutes or until the squash is tender and easily pierced with a fork.

VI.   Let the spaghetti squash cool for a few minutes, then use a fork to scrape the flesh into strands. Set aside.

VII.   In a large skillet, heat olive oil over medium heat.

VIII.   Add sliced red onion and minced garlic, sautéing until fragrant.

IX.   Add bell pepper, julienned zucchini, julienned carrot, cherry tomatoes, and broccoli florets to the skillet. Sauté for 5-7 minutes until the vegetables are tender-crisp.

X.   Add the spaghetti squash strands to the skillet, tossing everything together until well combined.

XI.   Season with salt and pepper to taste. Adjust seasoning as needed.

XII.   Stir in chopped fresh basil. Optionally, sprinkle with vegan Parmesan cheese and crushed red pepper flakes for added flavor.

XIII.   Serve the Spaghetti Squash Primavera warm as a healthy and low-carb alternative to traditional pasta dishes.

Estimated Nutritional Value (per serving)

Calories: 180, Protein: 4g, Fat: 10g, Carbohydrates: 22g, Fiber: 6g, Sugar: 8g

Tips

Customize with your favorite vegetables or seasonal produce.

Roast the spaghetti squash in advance for quicker preparation.

Experiment with different herbs and spices for varied flavor profiles.

Lentil and Vegetable Soup

 Prep Time: 45 minutes   Cook Time: 15 minutes

Ingredients

- 1 cup dried green or brown lentils, rinsed and drained

- 1 tablespoon olive oil

- 1 large onion, diced

- 2 carrots, diced

- 2 celery stalks, diced

- 3 cloves garlic, minced

- 1 teaspoon ground cumin

- 1 teaspoon ground coriander

- 1 teaspoon smoked paprika

- 1/2 teaspoon turmeric

- 1 bay leaf

- 6 cups vegetable broth

- 1 can (14 oz) diced tomatoes, undrained

- 2 cups kale or spinach, chopped

- Salt and pepper to taste

- Fresh lemon juice for serving

- Fresh parsley for garnish

Instructions

I.   In a large pot, heat olive oil over medium heat.

II. Add diced onion, carrots, and celery. Sauté until the vegetables are softened.

III. Add minced garlic, ground cumin, ground coriander, smoked paprika, turmeric, and the bay leaf. Sauté for an additional 2 minutes until fragrant.

IV. Add rinsed lentils to the pot and pour in the vegetable broth.

V. Bring the mixture to a boil, then reduce heat to simmer. Cover and cook for 25-30 minutes, or until lentils are tender.

VI. Stir in the diced tomatoes with their juice.

VII. Add chopped kale or spinach to the soup. Simmer for an additional 5-7 minutes until the greens are wilted.

VIII. Season the soup with salt and pepper to taste. Adjust seasoning as needed.

IX. Remove the bay leaf. Ladle the Lentil and Vegetable Soup into bowls.

X. Squeeze fresh lemon juice over each serving and garnish with chopped fresh parsley.

XI. Serve hot and enjoy your hearty and nutritious Lentil and Vegetable Soup!

Estimated Nutritional Value (per serving)

Calories: 250, Protein: 12g, Fat: 4g, Carbohydrates: 45g, Fiber: 15g, Sugar: 8g

Tips

Experiment with different varieties of lentils.

Customize with additional vegetables such as bell peppers or sweet potatoes.

Make a big batch and freeze for convenient future meals.

Quinoa and Black Bean Stuffed Peppers

 Prep Time: 40 minutes   Cook Time: 20 minutes

Ingredients

- 4 large bell peppers, halved and seeds removed

- 1 cup quinoa, rinsed and cooked according to package instructions

- 1 can (15 oz) black beans, drained and rinsed

- 1 cup corn kernels (fresh, frozen, or canned)

- 1 cup diced tomatoes

- 1 cup red onion, finely chopped

- 2 cloves garlic, minced

- 1 teaspoon ground cumin

- 1 teaspoon chili powder

- 1/2 teaspoon smoked paprika

- Salt and pepper to taste

- 1 cup tomato sauce

- 1 cup vegan shredded cheese (cheddar or Mexican blend)

- Fresh cilantro or parsley for garnish

Instructions

I. Preheat the oven to 375°F (190°C).

II. Cut the bell peppers in half lengthwise, removing the seeds and membranes.

III. Rinse quinoa under cold water. Cook according to package instructions.

IV. In a large bowl, combine cooked quinoa, black beans, corn, diced tomatoes, red onion, minced garlic, ground cumin, chili powder, smoked paprika, salt, and pepper. Mix well.

V.   Spoon the quinoa and black bean mixture into each bell pepper half, pressing down gently.

VI.   Pour tomato sauce over the stuffed peppers.

VII.   Sprinkle vegan shredded cheese over each stuffed pepper.

VIII.   Place the stuffed peppers in a baking dish and cover with aluminum foil.

IX.   Bake in the preheated oven for 30 minutes. Remove the foil and bake for an additional 10 minutes or until the cheese is melted and bubbly.

X.   Remove from the oven and garnish with fresh cilantro or parsley.

XI.   Serve the Quinoa and Black Bean Stuffed Peppers warm.

XII.

Estimated Nutritional Value (per serving - 1 stuffed pepper half)

Calories: 250, Protein: 10g, Fat: 5g, Carbohydrates: 45g, Fiber: 8g, Sugar: 8g

Tips

Customize the filling with additional vegetables like diced bell peppers or spinach.

Adjust the level of spice by adding more or less chili powder.

Use a variety of colored bell peppers for a visually appealing dish.

Baked Sweet Potato Falafel

 Prep Time: 30 minutes   Cook Time: 25 minutes

Ingredients

- 2 medium-sized sweet potatoes, peeled and cubed

- 1 can (15 oz) chickpeas, drained and rinsed

- 3 cloves garlic, minced

- 1/4 cup fresh cilantro, chopped

- 1/4 cup fresh parsley, chopped

- 1 teaspoon ground cumin

- 1 teaspoon ground coriander

- 1/2 teaspoon smoked paprika

- 1/2 teaspoon ground turmeric

- 1 tablespoon tahini

- Juice of 1 lemon

- 1/4 cup chickpea flour (or any flour of your choice)

- Salt and pepper to taste

- Olive oil for brushing

Instructions

I. Preheat the oven to 375°F (190°C).

II. Boil or steam the sweet potato cubes until they are fork-tender. Drain and let them cool.

III. In a food processor, combine sweet potatoes, chickpeas, minced garlic, cilantro, parsley, cumin, coriander, smoked paprika, turmeric, tahini, and lemon juice. Pulse until well combined but still slightly chunky.

IV.   Transfer the mixture to a bowl and add chickpea flour. Mix well. The mixture should be moldable and not too sticky. Add more flour if needed.

V.   Season the mixture with salt and pepper to taste. Adjust seasoning as needed.

VI.   Using your hands, shape the mixture into falafel-sized balls or patties and place them on a lined baking sheet.

VII.   Brush the tops of the falafel with olive oil.

VIII.   Bake in the preheated oven for 20-25 minutes or until the falafel is golden brown and firm to the touch.

IX.   Serve the Baked Sweet Potato Falafel warm.

Estimated Nutritional Value (per serving - 3 falafel)

Calories: 200, Protein: 6g, Fat: 5g, Carbohydrates: 35g, Fiber: 8g, Sugar: 6g

Tips

Ensure the sweet potatoes are well-cooked to easily mash and blend with other ingredients.

Experiment with different herbs and spices for varied flavor profiles.

Make a double batch and freeze the falafel for quick and convenient meals.

Coconut Curry Chickpeas

 Prep Time: 15 minutes   Cook Time: 30 minutes

Ingredients

- 2 cans (15 oz each) chickpeas, drained and rinsed
- 1 tablespoon coconut oil
- 1 large onion, finely chopped
- 3 cloves garlic, minced
- 1 tablespoon fresh ginger, grated
- 2 tablespoons curry powder
- 1 teaspoon ground cumin
- 1 teaspoon ground coriander
- 1/2 teaspoon turmeric

- 1/2 teaspoon red pepper flakes (adjust to taste)

- 1 can (14 oz) diced tomatoes, undrained

- 1 can (14 oz) coconut milk

- Salt and pepper to taste

- Fresh cilantro for garnish

- Cooked rice or naan for serving

Instructions

I. In a large skillet or pot, heat coconut oil over medium heat.

II. Add chopped onion, minced garlic, and grated ginger. Sauté until the onion is soft and translucent.

III. Stir in curry powder, ground cumin, ground coriander, turmeric, and red pepper flakes. Cook for an additional 1-2 minutes until the spices are fragrant.

IV.   Add drained and rinsed chickpeas to the skillet. Pour in diced tomatoes with their juice. Stir to combine.

V.   Pour in the coconut milk and season with salt and pepper. Bring the mixture to a simmer.

VI.   Reduce heat to low and let the curry simmer for about 15-20 minutes or until the sauce has thickened.

VII.   Garnish the Coconut Curry Chickpeas with fresh cilantro.

VIII.   Serve the curry over cooked rice or with naan bread.

Estimated Nutritional Value (per serving)

Calories: 350, Protein: 10g, Fat: 20g, Carbohydrates: 35g, Fiber: 8g, Sugar: 6g

Tips

Adjust the level of spiciness by adding more or less red pepper flakes.

Customize with additional vegetables such as spinach or bell peppers.

Experiment with different curry powders or pastes for varied flavor profiles.

Butternut Squash and Kale Salad

 Prep Time: 25 minutes   **Cook Time: 20 minutes**

Ingredients

- 1 small butternut squash, peeled, seeded, and diced

- 2 tablespoons olive oil

- 1 teaspoon maple syrup

- 1/2 teaspoon ground cinnamon

- Salt and pepper to taste

- 1 bunch kale, stems removed and leaves chopped

- 1/2 cup pecans, toasted and chopped

- 1/4 cup dried cranberries

- 1/4 cup vegan feta or goat cheese, crumbled

- Balsamic vinaigrette dressing (store-bought or homemade)

Instructions

I. Preheat the oven to 400°F (200°C).

II. In a large bowl, toss the diced butternut squash with olive oil, maple syrup, ground cinnamon, salt, and pepper.

III. Spread the squash evenly on a baking sheet.

IV. Roast in the preheated oven for 25 minutes or until the squash is tender and caramelized, stirring halfway through.

V. While the butternut squash is roasting, massage the chopped kale in a bowl with a bit of olive oil to soften the leaves.

VI. In a large serving bowl, combine the roasted butternut squash, massaged kale, toasted pecans, dried cranberries, and crumbled vegan feta or goat cheese.

VII. Drizzle the salad with balsamic vinaigrette dressing. Toss everything together until well coated.

VIII. Serve the Butternut Squash and Kale Salad as a delightful and hearty side dish.

Estimated Nutritional Value (per serving)

Calories: 250, Protein: 5g, Fat: 15g, Carbohydrates: 30g, Fiber: 5g, Sugar: 10g

Tips

Customize with your favorite nuts or seeds.

Swap dried cranberries for raisins or chopped apricots.

Make the salad in advance and refrigerate, allowing the flavors to meld.

Chickpea and Vegetable Stir-Fry

 Prep Time: 15 minutes   Cook Time: 15 minutes

Ingredients

- 1 can (15 oz) chickpeas, drained and rinsed

- 2 tablespoons soy sauce or tamari

- 1 tablespoon sesame oil

- 1 tablespoon olive oil

- 1 bell pepper, thinly sliced

- 1 carrot, julienned

- 1 cup snap peas, trimmed

- 1 cup broccoli florets

- 3 cloves garlic, minced

- 1 tablespoon fresh ginger, grated

- 1 teaspoon cornstarch (optional, for thickening)

- Green onions, sliced, for garnish

- Sesame seeds for garnish

- Cooked brown rice or quinoa for serving

Instructions

I.   In a bowl, toss chickpeas with soy sauce or tamari. Let them marinate for a few minutes.

II. Heat olive oil in a large skillet or wok over medium-high heat.

III. Add marinated chickpeas and stir-fry until golden and slightly crispy. Remove chickpeas from the skillet and set aside.

IV. In the same skillet, add sesame oil and sauté sliced bell pepper, julienned carrot, snap peas, and broccoli florets until they are crisp-tender.

V.   Return the stir-fried chickpeas to the skillet and toss with the vegetables.

VI.   Add minced garlic and grated ginger to the skillet. Sauté for an additional 1-2 minutes until fragrant.

VII.   If desired, mix cornstarch with a bit of water to create a slurry. Pour it into the skillet and stir to thicken the sauce.

VIII. Garnish the Chickpea and Vegetable Stir-Fry with sliced green onions and sesame seeds.

IX.   Serve over cooked brown rice or quinoa.

Estimated Nutritional Value (per serving)

Calories: 300, Protein: 12g, Fat: 8g, Carbohydrates: 45g, Fiber: 10g, Sugar: 8g

Tips

Use a variety of colorful vegetables for a visually appealing stir-fry.

Experiment with different sauces, such as hoisin or sweet chili sauce.

Ensure the skillet is hot before adding the chickpeas to achieve crispiness.

Mushroom and Spinach Quinoa Risotto

 Prep Time: 15 minutes   Cook Time: 30 minutes

Ingredients

- 1 cup quinoa, rinsed

- 2 tablespoons olive oil

- 1 onion, finely chopped

- 2 cloves garlic, minced

- 8 oz cremini or white mushrooms, sliced

- 2 cups baby spinach, chopped

- 1/2 cup dry white wine (optional)

- 4 cups vegetable broth, heated

- 1/2 cup vegan Parmesan cheese, grated

- Salt and pepper to taste

- Fresh parsley, chopped, for garnish

Instructions

I.   In a large saucepan, heat olive oil over medium heat. Add chopped onion and sauté until translucent.

II. Add sliced mushrooms and minced garlic to the saucepan. Sauté until the mushrooms release their moisture and become golden brown.

III. Stir in the rinsed quinoa and cook for 2-3 minutes, allowing it to toast slightly.

IV. If using wine, pour it into the saucepan and stir until it evaporates.

V.   Begin adding the heated vegetable broth one ladle at a time, stirring frequently. Allow the liquid to be absorbed before adding more.

VI. Continue this process until the quinoa is cooked and creamy, about 20 minutes.

VII.   In the last few minutes of cooking, fold in the chopped baby spinach until it wilts.

VIII. Stir in vegan Parmesan cheese and season with salt and pepper. Remove from heat.

IX.   Garnish the Mushroom and Spinach Quinoa Risotto with chopped fresh parsley.

X.   Serve warm, and enjoy this wholesome and flavorful risotto.

Estimated Nutritional Value (per serving)

Calories: 350, Protein: 12g, Fat: 12g, Carbohydrates: 45g, Fiber: 7g, Sugar: 2g

Tips

Stir the risotto frequently to achieve a creamy texture.

Experiment with different types of mushrooms for varied flavor profiles.

Use a high-quality vegetable broth for enhanced taste.

Sweet Potato and Lentil Curry

 Prep Time: 20 minutes   Cook Time: 35 minutes

Ingredients

- 1 cup dried green or brown lentils, rinsed and drained

- 2 medium-sized sweet potatoes, peeled and diced

- 1 tablespoon coconut oil

- 1 large onion, finely chopped

- 3 cloves garlic, minced

- 1 tablespoon fresh ginger, grated

- 2 tablespoons curry powder

- 1 teaspoon ground cumin

- 1 teaspoon ground coriander

- 1/2 teaspoon turmeric

- 1 can (14 oz) diced tomatoes, undrained

- 1 can (14 oz) coconut milk

- 3 cups vegetable broth

- Salt and pepper to taste

- Fresh cilantro for garnish

- Cooked basmati rice for serving

Instructions

I. In a large pot, heat coconut oil over medium heat. Add chopped onion, minced garlic, and grated ginger. Sauté until the onion is soft and translucent.

II. Stir in curry powder, ground cumin, ground coriander, and turmeric. Cook for an additional 2 minutes until the spices are fragrant.

III.   Add rinsed lentils, diced sweet potatoes, diced tomatoes with their juice, coconut milk, and vegetable broth to the pot. Stir to combine.

IV.   Bring the mixture to a boil, then reduce heat to simmer. Cover and cook for 25-30 minutes or until lentils and sweet potatoes are tender.

V.   Season the curry with salt and pepper to taste. Adjust seasoning as needed.

VI.   Garnish the Sweet Potato and Lentil Curry with fresh cilantro.

VII.   Serve over cooked basmati rice for a wholesome and satisfying meal.

Estimated Nutritional Value (per serving)

Calories: 400, Protein: 15g, Fat: 15g, Carbohydrates: 55g, Fiber: 12g, Sugar: 8g

Tips

Customize with additional vegetables such as spinach or bell peppers.

Adjust the level of spiciness by adding more or less curry powder.

Make a double batch and freeze for convenient future meals.

Mediterranean Zucchini Noodles

 Prep Time: 15 minutes   Cook Time: 5 minutes

Ingredients

- 4 medium-sized zucchinis, spiralized into noodles

- 2 tablespoons olive oil

- 3 cloves garlic, minced

- 1 cup cherry tomatoes, halved

- 1/2 cup Kalamata olives, pitted and sliced

- 1/4 cup fresh basil, chopped

- 1/4 cup fresh parsley, chopped

- Juice of 1 lemon

- Salt and pepper to taste

- Vegan feta cheese, crumbled, for garnish (optional)

Instructions

I. Using a spiralizer, create zucchini noodles and set aside.

II. In a large skillet, heat olive oil over medium heat. Add minced garlic and sauté until fragrant.

III. Add zucchini noodles to the skillet and toss to coat with the garlic-infused oil. Cook for 3-5 minutes or until the noodles are slightly tender.

IV. Add halved cherry tomatoes, sliced Kalamata olives, chopped fresh basil, and chopped fresh parsley to the skillet. Toss everything together until well combined.

V. Squeeze the juice of one lemon over the noodles. Season with salt and pepper to taste. Toss again to incorporate.

VI.   Garnish the Mediterranean Zucchini Noodles with crumbled vegan feta cheese, if desired.

VII.   Serve the zucchini noodles as a light and refreshing side dish.

Estimated Nutritional Value (per serving)

Calories: 150, Protein: 5g, Fat: 10g, Carbohydrates: 15g, Fiber: 5g, Sugar: 8g

Cilantro Lime Rice with Black Beans

 Prep Time: 10 minutes   Cook Time: 20 minutes

Ingredients

- 1 cup long-grain white rice

- 2 cups water

- 1 can (15 oz) black beans, drained and rinsed

- 1/4 cup fresh cilantro, chopped

- Juice of 2 limes

- 1 tablespoon olive oil

- Salt to taste

Instructions

I. In a saucepan, combine rice and water. Bring to a boil, then reduce heat to low, cover, and simmer for 15-20 minutes or until the rice is cooked and water is absorbed.

II. Once the rice is cooked, fluff it with a fork to separate the grains.

III. In a large bowl, combine the cooked rice with drained and rinsed black beans.

IV. Add chopped cilantro to the rice and beans. Squeeze the juice of two limes over the mixture.

V. Drizzle olive oil over the rice and beans. Toss everything together until well combined.

VI. Season the Cilantro Lime Rice with salt to taste. Adjust seasoning as needed.

VII. Serve the flavorful Cilantro Lime Rice with Black Beans as a side dish or base for your favorite Mexican-inspired toppings.

Estimated Nutritional Value (per serving)

Calories: 200, Protein: 5g, Fat: 3g, Carbohydrates: 40g, Fiber: 5g, Sugar: 1g

Tips

Use brown rice or quinoa for added nutritional benefits.

Customize with your favorite herbs or spices.

Make a larger batch for meal prep.

Eggplant and Tomato Casserole

 Prep Time: 20 minutes   Cook Time: 30 minutes

Ingredients

- 2 large eggplants, sliced into 1/2-inch rounds

- 2 tablespoons olive oil

- 1 onion, finely chopped

- 3 cloves garlic, minced

- 1 can (14 oz) diced tomatoes, drained

- 1/4 cup fresh basil, chopped

- 1/4 cup fresh parsley, chopped

- 1 teaspoon dried oregano

- Salt and pepper to taste

- 1 cup vegan mozzarella or Parmesan cheese, shredded

- 1/4 cup breadcrumbs (optional, for topping)

Instructions

I. Preheat the oven to 375°F (190°C).

II. Arrange eggplant slices on baking sheets. Brush both sides with olive oil. Roast in the preheated oven for 15-20 minutes or until golden brown.

III. In a skillet, heat olive oil over medium heat. Add chopped onion and minced garlic. Sauté until the onion is soft and translucent.

IV. Stir in drained diced tomatoes, chopped fresh basil, chopped fresh parsley, dried oregano, salt, and pepper. Cook for an additional 5 minutes.

V. In a baking dish, layer half of the roasted eggplant slices. Top with half of the tomato mixture. Repeat the layers.

VI.   Sprinkle shredded vegan mozzarella or Parmesan cheese over the top. If desired, add a layer of breadcrumbs for a crispy topping.

VII.   Bake in the preheated oven for 25-30 minutes or until the casserole is bubbly and the top is golden brown.

VIII.   Serve the Eggplant and Tomato Casserole as a savory and comforting dish.

Estimated Nutritional Value (per serving)

Calories: 250, Protein: 8g, Fat: 12g, Carbohydrates: 30g, Fiber: 10g, Sugar: 10g

Broccoli and Sun-Dried Tomato Pasta

 Prep Time: 15 minutes   Cook Time: 15 minutes

Ingredients

- 8 oz whole wheat or gluten-free pasta

- 2 cups broccoli florets

- 1/2 cup sun-dried tomatoes, sliced

- 3 tablespoons olive oil

- 3 cloves garlic, minced

- 1/4 teaspoon red pepper flakes (optional)

- Salt and black pepper to taste

- 1/4 cup fresh basil, chopped

- 1/4 cup vegan Parmesan cheese, grated (optional)

Instructions

I.   Cook the pasta according to package instructions in a large pot of salted boiling water. Add the broccoli to the boiling water during the last 3 minutes of pasta cooking time.

II. In a large skillet, heat olive oil over medium heat. Add minced garlic and red pepper flakes (if using). Sauté for 1-2 minutes until the garlic is fragrant.

III. Stir in sliced sun-dried tomatoes and cook for an additional 2 minutes.

IV. Drain the cooked pasta and broccoli, reserving a cup of pasta water. Add the pasta and broccoli to the skillet with the sun-dried tomatoes and toss to combine.

V.   Season the Broccoli and Sun-Dried Tomato Pasta with salt and black pepper to taste. Adjust seasoning as needed.

VI. Stir in chopped fresh basil. If desired, sprinkle vegan Parmesan cheese over the top.

VII. Serve the flavorful pasta warm, garnished with additional basil and a drizzle of olive oil.

Estimated Nutritional Value (per serving)

Calories: 400, Protein: 15g, Fat: 12g, Carbohydrates: 60g, Fiber: 8g, Sugar: 5g

Tips

Use your favorite type of pasta, whether it's penne, fusilli, or spaghetti.

Customize with additional vegetables such as cherry tomatoes or spinach.

Experiment with different varieties of sun-dried tomatoes for varied flavor profiles.

Avocado and Chickpea Salad

 Prep Time: 15 minutes   Cook Time: 0 minutes

Ingredients

- 2 cans (15 oz each) chickpeas, drained and rinsed

- 2 ripe avocados, diced

- 1 cup cherry tomatoes, halved

- 1/2 cucumber, diced

- 1/4 cup red onion, finely chopped

- 1/4 cup fresh cilantro, chopped

- Juice of 2 limes

- 2 tablespoons olive oil

- Salt and black pepper to taste

- 1/2 teaspoon cumin (optional)

- 1/4 cup pumpkin seeds (pepitas) for garnish

Instructions

I. In a large bowl, combine drained and rinsed chickpeas with diced avocados, halved cherry tomatoes, diced cucumber, chopped red onion, and chopped cilantro.

II. In a small bowl, whisk together the lime juice, olive oil, salt, black pepper, and cumin (if using).

III. Pour the dressing over the chickpea mixture. Toss everything together until well coated.

IV. Garnish the Avocado and Chickpea Salad with pumpkin seeds.

V. Serve the refreshing salad immediately or refrigerate until ready to serve.

Estimated Nutritional Value (per serving)

Calories: 350, Protein: 10g, Fat: 20g, Carbohydrates: 35g, Fiber: 12g, Sugar: 5g

Tips

Customize with additional vegetables such as bell peppers or radishes.

Adjust the level of acidity by adding more or less lime juice.

Make a larger batch and store in an airtight container for a quick and healthy lunch.

CHAPTER FOUR

Snack and Appetizer Recipes

Roasted Red Pepper Hummus Cucumber and Carrot Sticks with

 Prep Time: 15 minutes   Roasting Time: 0 minutes

Ingredients

- 1 can (15 oz) chickpeas, drained and rinsed

- 1/2 cup roasted red peppers (store-bought or homemade)

- 1/4 cup tahini

- 2 cloves garlic, minced

- Juice of 1 lemon

- 3 tablespoons olive oil

- 1/2 teaspoon ground cumin

- Salt and pepper to taste

- Paprika for garnish

- Pita bread or vegetable sticks for dipping

Instructions

1. If using fresh red peppers, roast them in the oven or over an open flame until charred. Peel, remove seeds, and set aside.

2. In a food processor, combine chickpeas, roasted red peppers, tahini, minced garlic, lemon juice, olive oil, ground cumin, salt, and pepper.

3. Blend the ingredients until smooth and creamy. If the consistency is too thick, add a bit of water or extra olive oil.

4. Taste the Roasted Red Pepper Hummus and adjust the seasoning as needed.

5. Transfer the hummus to a serving bowl. Drizzle with olive oil, sprinkle paprika for garnish, and serve with pita bread or vegetable sticks.

Estimated Nutritional Value (per serving)

Calories: 150, Protein: 5g, Fat: 10g, Carbohydrates: 15g, Fiber: 4g, Sugar: 2g

Tips

Experiment with different variations, such as adding roasted garlic or smoked paprika.

Make a big batch and refrigerate for quick and easy snacking.

Customize the texture by adjusting the amount of liquid added.

Cucumber and Carrot Sticks with Guacamole

 Prep Time: 15 minutes   Cook Time: 0 minutes

Ingredients

- 2 ripe avocados

- 1 lime, juiced

- 1/4 cup red onion, finely chopped

- 1/4 cup fresh cilantro, chopped

- 1 clove garlic, minced

- Salt and pepper to taste

- 2 medium cucumbers, cut into sticks

- 4 medium carrots, peeled and cut into sticks

Instructions

1. In a bowl, mash the ripe avocados with a fork. Add lime juice, chopped red onion, chopped cilantro, minced garlic, salt, and pepper.

2. Mix the ingredients until well combined. Taste and adjust the seasoning as needed.

3. Cut the cucumbers and carrots into sticks.

4. Arrange the cucumber and carrot sticks on a serving platter. Place the bowl of guacamole in the center.

5. Dip the cucumber and carrot sticks into the guacamole and enjoy this fresh and healthy snack.

Estimated Nutritional Value (per serving)

Calories: 200, Protein: 3g, Fat: 15g, Carbohydrates: 20g, Fiber: 10g, Sugar: 5g

Tips

For extra flavor, add diced tomatoes or corn to the guacamole.

Make the guacamole just before serving to preserve its freshness.

Encourage creativity by offering a variety of dipping options like bell pepper strips or jicama sticks.

Baked Plantain Chips

 Prep Time: 10 minutes   **Baking Time: 20 minutes**

Ingredients

- 2 green plantains, peeled

- 2 tablespoons olive oil

- 1 teaspoon smoked paprika

- 1/2 teaspoon garlic powder

- 1/2 teaspoon sea salt

- Pinch of cayenne pepper (optional)

Instructions

1. Preheat the oven to 400°F (200°C) and line a baking sheet with parchment paper.

2. Using a sharp knife or a mandoline slicer, thinly slice the peeled plantains.

3. In a bowl, toss the plantain slices with olive oil, smoked paprika, garlic powder, sea salt, and cayenne pepper (if using). Ensure the slices are evenly coated.

4. Arrange the seasoned plantain slices in a single layer on the prepared baking sheet.

5. Bake in the preheated oven for 15-20 minutes, flipping the slices halfway through, or until the plantains are golden brown and crisp.

6. Allow the Baked Plantain Chips to cool before serving. They will continue to crisp up as they cool.

Estimated Nutritional Value (per serving)

Calories: 150, Protein: 1g, Fat: 7g, Carbohydrates: 22g, Fiber: 2g, Sugar: 8g

Tips

Choose green plantains for a firmer texture.

Experiment with different seasonings like cinnamon or chili powder.

Keep an eye on them while baking to prevent burning.

Olive and Tomato Tapenade

 Prep Time: 10 minutes　　 Cook Time: 0 minutes

Ingredients

- 1 cup Kalamata olives, pitted

- 1 cup cherry tomatoes, quartered

- 2 tablespoons capers, drained

- 2 cloves garlic, minced

- 2 tablespoons fresh basil, chopped

- 1 tablespoon fresh lemon juice

- 3 tablespoons extra-virgin olive oil

- Salt and black pepper to taste

- Baguette slices or crackers for serving

Instructions

I. Pit the Kalamata olives and quarter the cherry tomatoes.

II. In a food processor, combine pitted Kalamata olives, quartered cherry tomatoes, drained capers, minced garlic, chopped fresh basil, fresh lemon juice, and extra-virgin olive oil.

III. Pulse the ingredients in the food processor until the mixture reaches your desired consistency. You can keep it slightly chunky or make it smoother.

IV. Taste the Olive and Tomato Tapenade and season with salt and black pepper as needed.

V. Transfer the tapenade to a serving bowl and serve with baguette slices or crackers.

Estimated Nutritional Value (per serving)

Calories: 120, Protein: 1g, Fat: 12g, Carbohydrates: 4g, Fiber: 1g, Sugar: 1g

Tips

Experiment with different olive varieties for varied flavor profiles.

Add a pinch of crushed red pepper for a spicy kick.

Refrigerate any leftovers; the flavors may intensify over time.

Sweet Potato and Beet Chips

 Prep Time: 15 minutes   **Baking Time: 20 minutes**

Ingredients

- 2 medium-sized sweet potatoes, peeled

- 2 medium-sized beets, peeled

- 2 tablespoons olive oil

- 1 teaspoon smoked paprika

- 1/2 teaspoon garlic powder

- 1/2 teaspoon sea salt

- Fresh thyme leaves for garnish

Instructions

I.   Preheat the oven to 375°F (190°C) and line two baking sheets with parchment paper.

II.   Using a mandolin slicer or a sharp knife, thinly slice the peeled sweet potatoes and beets.

III.   In a bowl, toss the sweet potato and beet slices with olive oil, smoked paprika, garlic powder, and sea salt. Ensure the slices are evenly coated.

IV.   Arrange the seasoned sweet potato and beet slices in a single layer on the prepared baking sheets, ensuring they are not overlapping.

V.   Bake in the preheated oven for 20-25 minutes or until the chips are golden brown and crisp. Rotate the trays halfway through the baking time.

VI.   Allow the Sweet Potato and Beet Chips to cool on the baking sheets. Garnish with fresh thyme leaves before serving.

Estimated Nutritional Value (per serving)

Calories: 120, Protein: 2g, Fat: 7g, Carbohydrates: 15g, Fiber: 3g, Sugar: 5g

Tips

Keep an eye on them while baking to prevent burning.

Experiment with different root vegetables like parsnips or turnips.

Store in an airtight container to maintain crispiness.

Edamame and Sesame Salad

 Prep Time: 10 minutes   Cook Time: 0 minutes

Ingredients

- 2 cups frozen edamame, thawed

- 1 cup cherry tomatoes, halved

- 1/4 cup red onion, finely chopped

- 2 tablespoons sesame seeds

- 2 tablespoons soy sauce (or tamari for gluten-free)

- 1 tablespoon rice vinegar

- 1 tablespoon sesame oil

- 1 teaspoon agave syrup or maple syrup

- 1/2 teaspoon grated ginger

- 1 clove garlic, minced

- Fresh cilantro for garnish

Instructions

I. If using frozen edamame, cook according to package instructions. Allow to cool.

II. In a large bowl, combine thawed edamame, halved cherry tomatoes, chopped red onion, and sesame seeds.

III. In a small bowl, whisk together soy sauce, rice vinegar, sesame oil, agave syrup or maple syrup, grated ginger, and minced garlic.

IV. Pour the dressing over the Edamame and Sesame Salad. Toss until well coated.

V. Garnish the salad with fresh cilantro.

VI. Serve the refreshing Edamame and Sesame Salad immediately or refrigerate until ready to serve.

Estimated Nutritional Value (per serving)

Calories: 180, Protein: 12g, Fat: 10g, Carbohydrates: 15g, Fiber: 6g, Sugar: 5g

Tips

Use shelled edamame for convenience.

Customize with additional vegetables such as cucumber or bell peppers.

Make ahead of time for a quick and healthy grab-and-go option.

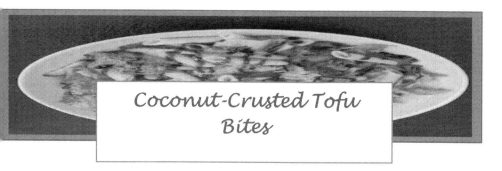

Coconut-Crusted Tofu Bites

 Prep Time: 15 minutes   Baking Time: 25 minutes

Ingredients

- 1 block extra-firm tofu, pressed and cut into bite-sized cubes

- 1 cup unsweetened shredded coconut

- 1/2 cup almond flour

- 1 teaspoon garlic powder

- 1/2 teaspoon smoked paprika

- 1/2 teaspoon sea salt

- 1/4 teaspoon black pepper

- 2 flax eggs (2 tablespoons ground flaxseed + 6 tablespoons water)

- Cooking spray or olive oil for greasing

Instructions

I. Preheat the oven to 375°F (190°C) and line a baking sheet with parchment paper.

II. In a small bowl, combine ground flaxseed and water to make two flax eggs. Let it sit for 5 minutes until it thickens.

III. In a shallow dish, combine shredded coconut, almond flour, garlic powder, smoked paprika, sea salt, and black pepper.

IV. Dip each tofu cube into the flax eggs, ensuring it is fully coated, then roll it in the coconut mixture, pressing gently to adhere.

V. Place the coated tofu cubes on the prepared baking sheet in a single layer.

VI.   Bake in the preheated oven for 25 minutes or until the coconut coating is golden brown and the tofu is crisp.

VII.   Allow the Coconut-Crusted Tofu Bites to cool slightly before serving.

Estimated Nutritional Value (per serving)

Calories: 200, Protein: 10g, Fat: 15g, Carbohydrates: 10g, Fiber: 5g, Sugar: 1g

Tips

For extra crispiness, flip the tofu cubes halfway through baking.

Customize the seasoning with your favorite herbs or spices.

Make a larger batch and freeze for convenient future use.

Avocado Salsa

 Prep Time: 15 minutes   Cook Time: 0 minutes

Ingredients

- 2 ripe avocados, diced

- 1 cup cherry tomatoes, diced

- 1/4 cup red onion, finely chopped

- 1/4 cup fresh cilantro, chopped

- 1 jalapeño, seeded and minced

- Juice of 2 limes

- Salt and black pepper to taste

- Tortilla chips or sliced veggies for serving

Instructions

I. Dice the avocados, cherry tomatoes, and red onion. Chop fresh cilantro and seed and mince the jalapeño.

II. In a bowl, combine diced avocados, diced cherry tomatoes, chopped red onion, chopped cilantro, minced jalapeño, and lime juice.

III. Season the Avocado Salsa with salt and black pepper to taste. Gently toss to combine.

IV. Serve the refreshing Avocado Salsa with tortilla chips or sliced veggies.

Estimated Nutritional Value (per serving)

Calories: 150, Protein: 2g, Fat: 12g, Carbohydrates: 12g, Fiber: 7g, Sugar: 2g

Tips

Adjust the level of spiciness by adding more or less jalapeño.

For extra flavor, add a dash of cumin or chili powder.

Make just before serving to maintain the vibrant color and freshness.

Spinach Artichoke Dip (Dairy-Free)

 Prep Time: 15 minutes　　Baking Time: 25 minutes

Ingredients

- 1 cup raw cashews, soaked in hot water for 1 hour

- 1 cup unsweetened almond milk

- 1 tablespoon nutritional yeast

- 2 cloves garlic, minced

- 1 tablespoon lemon juice

- 1/2 teaspoon onion powder

- 1/2 teaspoon sea salt

- 1/4 teaspoon black pepper

- 2 cups fresh spinach, chopped

- 1 can (14 oz) artichoke hearts, drained and chopped
- 1/4 cup vegan Parmesan cheese, grated
- 1/4 cup vegan mozzarella cheese, shredded
- Olive oil for greasing
- Tortilla chips or sliced veggies for serving

Instructions

I. Preheat the oven to 375°F (190°C) and lightly grease a baking dish with olive oil.

II. In a blender, combine soaked cashews, almond milk, nutritional yeast, minced garlic, lemon juice, onion powder, sea salt, and black pepper. Blend until smooth and creamy.

III. In a skillet, sauté chopped spinach and artichoke hearts until the spinach is wilted and the artichokes are softened.

IV. In a large bowl, mix the sautéed spinach and artichokes with the cashew cream. Add vegan Parmesan and mozzarella cheese. Stir until well combined.

V. Transfer the mixture to the prepared baking dish. Bake in the preheated oven for 25 minutes or until the top is golden and bubbly.

VI. Allow the Dairy-Free Spinach Artichoke Dip to cool slightly before serving. Serve with tortilla chips or sliced veggies.

Estimated Nutritional Value (per serving)

Calories: 150, Protein: 5g, Fat: 10g, Carbohydrates: 12g, Fiber: 3g, Sugar: 2g

Tips

Adjust the consistency by adding more or less almond milk.

Customize with additional spices like smoked paprika or cayenne.

Make the cashew cream in advance for quicker preparation.

Roasted Brussels Sprouts with Balsamic Glaze:

 Prep Time: 10 minutes   **Roasting Time: 25 minutes**

Ingredients

- 1 lb Brussels sprouts, trimmed and halved

- 2 tablespoons olive oil

- 2 tablespoons balsamic vinegar

- 1 tablespoon maple syrup

- 1/2 teaspoon sea salt

- 1/4 teaspoon black pepper

- 1/4 cup chopped pecans (optional, for garnish)

Instructions

I.   Preheat the oven to 400°F (200°C) and line a baking sheet with parchment paper.

II.   Prepare Brussels Sprouts:

III. Trim the ends of Brussels sprouts and cut them in half.

IV.   In a small bowl, whisk together olive oil, balsamic vinegar, maple syrup, sea salt, and black pepper.

V.   Toss the halved Brussels sprouts in the balsamic glaze mixture until well coated.

VI.   Spread the Brussels sprouts in a single layer on the prepared baking sheet. Roast in the preheated oven for 25 minutes or until they are golden brown and crispy at the edges.

VII. Optional: Garnish the Roasted Brussels Sprouts with chopped pecans before serving.

Estimated Nutritional Value (per serving)

Calories: 120, Protein: 3g, Fat: 7g, Carbohydrates: 14g, Fiber: 4g, Sugar: 6g

Tips

Ensure Brussels sprouts are evenly coated in the balsamic glaze for balanced flavor.

Experiment with different nuts such as walnuts or almonds.

Roast until the outer leaves are crispy for the best texture.

Stuffed Grape Leaves with Quinoa

 Prep Time: 30 minutes   Cook Time: 30 minutes

Ingredients

- 1 cup quinoa, rinsed

- 2 cups vegetable broth

- 1/2 cup chia, toasted

- 1/4 cup fresh parsley, chopped

- 1/4 cup fresh mint, chopped

- 1/4 cup dried currants or raisins

- 1/4 cup sun-dried tomatoes, finely chopped

- 1/4 cup extra-virgin olive oil

- Juice of 1 lemon

- Salt and black pepper to taste

- 1 jar grape leaves in brine, drained

- Greek yogurt or tahini sauce for serving

Instructions

I. In a medium saucepan, combine quinoa and vegetable broth. Bring to a boil, then reduce heat, cover, and simmer for 15-20 minutes or until quinoa is cooked and liquid is absorbed.

II. In a dry skillet, toast chia seeds over medium heat until golden brown. Set aside.

III. In a large bowl, combine cooked quinoa, toasted pine nuts, chopped parsley, chopped mint, currants or raisins, chopped sun-dried tomatoes, olive oil, and lemon juice. Mix well.

IV. Season the quinoa mixture with salt and black pepper to taste. Adjust seasoning as needed.

V.   Gently separate grape leaves and place them shiny side down on a clean surface. Trim any stems.

VI.   Place a grape leaf on a flat surface. Add a tablespoon of the quinoa mixture near the stem end. Fold the sides in and roll tightly.

VII. Arrange the stuffed grape leaves in a wide pot, seam side down, in a single layer.

VIII. Add enough water to the pot to cover the grape leaves. Cover and simmer over low heat for 30 minutes.

IX.   Allow the Stuffed Grape Leaves with Quinoa to cool before serving. Serve with Greek yogurt or tahini sauce.

Estimated Nutritional Value (per serving)

Calories: 200, Protein: 5g, Fat: 12g, Carbohydrates: 20g, Fiber: 3g, Sugar: 2g

Tips

Adjust the filling to your taste preferences by adding more herbs or dried fruits.

Store leftovers in the refrigerator; they can be enjoyed cold or reheated.

Practice rolling a few grape leaves to get the hang of it before assembling a larger batch.

Almond and Seed Energy Bites

 Prep Time: 15 minutes   Chilling Time: 15 minutes

Ingredients

- 1 cup rolled oats

- 1/2 cup almond butter

- 1/4 cup honey or maple syrup

- 1/4 cup ground flaxseed

- 1/4 cup chia seeds

- 1/4 cup pumpkin seeds

- 1/4 cup chopped almonds

- 1 teaspoon vanilla extract

- Pinch of salt

- Shredded coconut for rolling (optional)

Instructions

I.   In a large bowl, mix together rolled oats, almond butter, honey or maple syrup, ground flaxseed, chia seeds, pumpkin seeds, chopped almonds, vanilla extract, and a pinch of salt.

II. Place the mixture in the refrigerator for at least 30 minutes to firm up.

III. Once chilled, use your hands to shape the mixture into bite-sized balls. If desired, roll the energy bites in shredded coconut.

IV. Place the formed energy bites back in the refrigerator for an additional 15-20 minutes to set.

V.   Serve the Almond and Seed Energy Bites immediately or store in an airtight container in the refrigerator.

Estimated Nutritional Value (per serving)

Calories: 150, Protein: 4g, Fat: 9g, Carbohydrates: 15g, Fiber: 3g, Sugar: 6g

Tips

Adjust sweetness by adding more or less honey or maple syrup.

Experiment with different nut butters like peanut butter or sunflower seed butter.

Store in the refrigerator for a longer shelf life.

Guilt-Free Popcorn with Nutritional Yeast

 Prep Time: 10 minutes   Cook Time: 5 minutes

Ingredients

- 1/2 cup popcorn kernels

- 2 tablespoons nutritional yeast

- 1 tablespoon olive oil

- 1/2 teaspoon garlic powder

- 1/2 teaspoon onion powder

- Salt to taste

Instructions

I.   Using an air popper or stovetop method, pop the popcorn kernels. Place the popped popcorn in a large bowl.

II.   In a small bowl, mix nutritional yeast, olive oil, garlic powder, onion powder, and salt.

III. Drizzle the nutritional yeast mixture over the popped popcorn while tossing to ensure even coating.

IV.   Toss the popcorn until well coated with the nutritional yeast mixture. Adjust salt to taste.

V.   Guilt-Free Popcorn with Nutritional Yeast is ready to enjoy as a healthy and flavorful snack.

Estimated Nutritional Value (per serving)

Calories: 100, Protein: 2g, Fat: 4g, Carbohydrates: 14g, Fiber: 3g, Sugar: 0g

Tips

Use an air popper for a lower calorie option.

Experiment with different seasoning variations for added flavor.

Make a large batch and store in an airtight container for future snacking.

Crispy Baked Kale Chips

 Prep Time: 10 minutes   **Baking Time: 15 minutes**

Ingredients

- 1 bunch kale, stems removed and torn into bite-sized pieces
- 1 tablespoon olive oil
- 1 teaspoon nutritional yeast
- 1/2 teaspoon garlic powder
- 1/2 teaspoon onion powder
- 1/4 teaspoon smoked paprika
- Salt and black pepper to taste

Instructions

I.   Preheat the oven to 325°F (163°C) and line a baking sheet with parchment paper.

II.   Remove the stems from the kale leaves and tear the leaves into bite-sized pieces.

III.   In a large bowl, massage the kale pieces with olive oil until well coated.

IV.   Sprinkle nutritional yeast, garlic powder, onion powder, smoked paprika, salt, and black pepper over the kale. Toss to evenly distribute the seasonings.

V.   Spread the seasoned kale pieces on the prepared baking sheet in a single layer.

VI.   Bake in the preheated oven for 12-15 minutes or until the kale is crisp but not browned.

VII.   Allow the Crispy Baked Kale Chips to cool on the baking sheet before serving.

Estimated Nutritional Value (per serving)

Calories: 50, Protein: 2g, Fat: 3g, Carbohydrates: 6g, Fiber: 2g, Sugar: 0g

Tips

Ensure the kale is dry before massaging with oil for extra crispiness.

Experiment with different seasonings like cumin or chili powder.

Watch closely while baking to prevent burning.

Mixed Berry Smoothie Bowl

 Prep Time: 10 minutes   Cook Time: 0 minutes

- **Ingredients**

- 1 cup frozen mixed berries (strawberries, blueberries, raspberries)

- 1 frozen banana, sliced

- 1/2 cup unsweetened almond milk

- 1 tablespoon chia seeds

- 1 tablespoon almond butter

- Toppings: Fresh berries, sliced banana, granola, shredded coconut, chia seeds

Instructions

I. In a blender, combine frozen mixed berries, frozen banana slices, almond milk, chia seeds, and almond butter. Blend until smooth and creamy.

II. Pour the smoothie into a bowl.

III. Top the smoothie bowl with fresh berries, sliced banana, granola, shredded coconut, and additional chia seeds.

IV. Dig in and enjoy the refreshing and nutritious Mixed Berry Smoothie Bowl!

Estimated Nutritional Value (per serving)

Calories: 250, Protein: 5g, Fat: 10g, Carbohydrates: 40g, Fiber: 10g, Sugar: 15g

Tips

Experiment with different frozen fruits for variety.

Adjust the thickness by adding more or less almond milk.

Freeze leftover smoothie into popsicle molds for a frozen treat.

Quinoa Salad with Lemon Vinaigrette

 Prep Time: 15 minutes   Cook Time: 15 minutes

Ingredients

- 1 cup quinoa, rinsed

- 2 cups water or vegetable broth

- 1 cup cherry tomatoes, halved

- 1 cucumber, diced

- 1 bell pepper, diced (any color)

- 1/4 cup red onion, finely chopped

- 1/4 cup Kalamata olives, pitted and sliced

- 1/4 cup fresh parsley, chopped

- 1/4 cup feta cheese, crumbled (optional)

- Salt and black pepper to taste

Lemon Vinaigrette:

- 1/4 cup extra-virgin olive oil

- 2 tablespoons fresh lemon juice

- 1 teaspoon Dijon mustard

- 1 clove garlic, minced

- 1 teaspoon honey or maple syrup

- Salt and black pepper to taste

Instructions

I.   In a saucepan, combine quinoa and water or vegetable broth. Bring to a boil, then reduce heat, cover, and simmer for 15 minutes or until quinoa is cooked and liquid is absorbed. Fluff with a fork and let it cool.

II. In a small bowl, whisk together olive oil, fresh lemon juice, Dijon mustard, minced garlic, honey or maple syrup, salt, and black pepper to make the lemon vinaigrette.

III. In a large bowl, combine cooked quinoa, cherry tomatoes, cucumber, bell pepper, red onion, Kalamata olives, and fresh parsley.

IV. If using, add crumbled feta cheese to the salad.

V. Drizzle the lemon vinaigrette over the salad and toss until well combined.

VI. Season the Quinoa Salad with Salt and black pepper to taste. Adjust seasoning as needed.

VII. Refrigerate the salad for at least 30 minutes before serving to allow flavors to meld. Serve chilled.

Estimated Nutritional Value (per serving)

Calories: 250, Protein: 7g, Fat: 12g, Carbohydrates: 30g, Fiber: 5g. Sugar: 3g

Tips

Customize the salad with your favorite vegetables.

Make extra vinaigrette and store it separately for later use.

For a vegan version, omit the feta cheese or use a plant-based alternative.

Roasted Vegetable Medley
Cabbage and Carrot Slaw

 Prep Time: 15 minutes   Roasting Time: 25 minutes

Ingredients

- 1 cup cherry tomatoes, halved

- 1 zucchini, sliced

- 1 yellow bell pepper, sliced

- 1 red onion, sliced

- 1 cup baby carrots, halved

- 2 tablespoons olive oil

- 1 teaspoon dried thyme

- 1 teaspoon dried rosemary

- 1 teaspoon garlic powder

- Salt and black pepper to taste

- Fresh parsley for garnish (optional)

Instructions

I. Preheat the oven to 400°F (200°C) and line a baking sheet with parchment paper.

II. In a large bowl, combine cherry tomatoes, zucchini, yellow bell pepper, red onion, and baby carrots.

III. Drizzle olive oil over the vegetables and toss to coat evenly.

IV. Sprinkle dried thyme, dried rosemary, garlic powder, salt, and black pepper over the vegetables. Toss again to distribute the seasonings.

V. Spread the seasoned vegetables on the prepared baking sheet in a single layer.

VI.   Roast in the preheated oven for 25 minutes or until the vegetables are tender and lightly browned.

VII.   Optional: Garnish the Roasted Vegetable Medley with fresh parsley before serving.

Estimated Nutritional Value (per serving)

Calories: 120, Protein: 2g, Fat: 7g, Carbohydrates: 14g, Fiber: 4g, Sugar: 6g

Tips

Experiment with your favorite vegetables or those in season.

Ensure even roasting by spreading the vegetables in a single layer on the baking sheet.

Customize the seasoning to your taste preferences.

Cabbage and Carrot Slaw:

 Prep Time: 15 minutes   Cook Time: 0 minutes

Ingredients

- 2 cups shredded green cabbage

- 1 cup shredded carrots

- 1/4 cup thinly sliced red onion

- 1/4 cup chopped fresh cilantro

- 1/4 cup mayonnaise (dairy-free if needed)

- 2 tablespoons apple cider vinegar

- 1 tablespoon Dijon mustard

- 1 tablespoon maple syrup or honey

- Salt and black pepper to taste

Instructions

I. In a large bowl, combine shredded green cabbage, shredded carrots, sliced red onion, and chopped cilantro.

II. In a small bowl, whisk together mayonnaise, apple cider vinegar, Dijon mustard, and maple syrup or honey to create the dressing.

III. Pour the dressing over the cabbage and carrot mixture. Toss until the vegetables are evenly coated with the dressing.

IV. Season the Cabbage and Carrot Slaw with salt and black pepper to taste. Adjust seasoning as needed.

V. Refrigerate the slaw for at least 30 minutes before serving to allow the flavors to meld. Serve chilled.

Estimated Nutritional Value (per serving)

Calories: 120m Protein: 1g, Fat: 8g, Carbohydrates: 12g, Fiber: 3g, Sugar: 7g

Tips

Add sliced apples or raisins for a touch of sweetness.

Customize the dressing by adding a pinch of celery seed or poppy seeds.

Make the slaw in advance for a convenient and quick side dish.

Grilled Asparagus with Lemon Zest

 Prep Time: 10 minutes　　 **Grill Time: 5-7 minutes**

Ingredients

- 1 bunch asparagus, woody ends trimmed

- 1 tablespoon olive oil

- 1 teaspoon lemon zest

- 1 clove garlic, minced

- Salt and black pepper to taste

- Lemon wedges for serving

Instructions

I.   Preheat the grill to medium-high heat.

II.   In a large bowl, toss the trimmed asparagus with olive oil, lemon zest, minced garlic, salt, and black pepper.

III. Place the asparagus on the preheated grill. Grill for 5-7 minutes, turning occasionally, until the asparagus is tender and has grill marks.

IV.   Transfer the grilled asparagus to a serving platter. Squeeze fresh lemon juice over the top before serving.

Estimated Nutritional Value (per serving)

Calories: 50, Protein: 2g, Fat: 3g, Carbohydrates: 5g, Fiber: 3g, Sugar: 2g

Tips

Trim the woody ends of the asparagus for better texture.

Adjust grilling time based on the thickness of the asparagus spears.

Grill on a grill pan if an outdoor grill is not available.

Caprese Salad with Dairy-Free Mozzarella

 Prep Time: 15 minutes   Cook Time: 0 minutes

Ingredients

- 2 cups cherry tomatoes, halved

- 1 cup dairy-free mozzarella cheese, cubed

- 1/4 cup fresh basil leaves, torn

- 2 tablespoons balsamic glaze

- 1 tablespoon extra-virgin olive oil

- Salt and black pepper to taste

Instructions

I.   In a large bowl, combine halved cherry tomatoes, dairy-free mozzarella cheese cubes, and torn fresh basil leaves.

II. In a small bowl, whisk together balsamic glaze and extra-virgin olive oil to create the dressing.

III. Drizzle the balsamic glaze dressing over the tomato and mozzarella mixture.

IV. Season the Caprese Salad with salt and black pepper to taste. Gently toss to combine.

V. Refrigerate the salad for at least 15 minutes to allow the flavors to meld. Serve chilled.

Estimated Nutritional Value (per serving)

Calories: 150, Protein: 5g, Fat: 10g, Carbohydrates: 10g, Fiber: 2g, Sugar: 5g

Tips

Choose a high-quality dairy-free mozzarella for better texture and flavor.

Use a balsamic glaze with a thicker consistency for better drizzling.

Freshly picked and ripe tomatoes enhance the salad's overall taste.

Mediterranean Chickpea Salad

 Prep Time: 15 minutes   **Cook Time: 0 minutes**

Prep Time: 15 minutes

Ingredients

- 2 cans (15 oz each) chickpeas, drained and rinsed

- 1 cup cherry tomatoes, halved

- 1 cucumber, diced

- 1/2 red onion, finely chopped

- 1/2 cup Kalamata olives, pitted and sliced

- 1/2 cup fresh parsley, chopped

- 1/4 cup fresh mint, chopped

- 1/2 cup feta cheese, crumbled (optional, omit for

  dairy-free version)

Lemon Herb Dressing

- 1/4 cup extra-virgin olive oil

- 2 tablespoons fresh lemon juice

- 1 teaspoon dried oregano

- 1 teaspoon ground cumin

- Salt and black pepper to taste

Instructions

I.   In a large bowl, combine chickpeas, cherry tomatoes, diced cucumber, finely chopped red onion, sliced Kalamata olives, fresh parsley, and fresh mint.

II. In a small bowl, whisk together extra-virgin olive oil, fresh lemon juice, dried oregano, ground cumin, salt, and black pepper to create the lemon herb dressing.

III. Drizzle the lemon herb dressing over the chickpea mixture. Toss until all ingredients are well coated.

IV. If using, add crumbled feta cheese to the salad and toss gently.

V. Refrigerate the Mediterranean Chickpea Salad for at least 30 minutes before serving to enhance the flavors. Serve chilled.

Estimated Nutritional Value (per serving)

Calories: 250, Protein: 9g, Fat: 14g, Carbohydrates: 26g, Fiber: 8g, Sugar: 5g

Tips

Customize with additional vegetables like bell peppers or artichoke hearts.

Make it vegan by omitting the feta cheese or using a dairy-free alternative.

Adjust the dressing ingredients to suit your taste preferences.

Beet and Orange Salad

🕐 Prep Time: 20 minutes   👨‍🍳 Cook Time: 0 minutes

Ingredients

- 4 medium beets, cooked, peeled, and sliced

- 2 large oranges, peeled and segmented

- 1/4 cup red onion, thinly sliced

- 1/4 cup fresh mint leaves, torn

- 1/4 cup crumbled goat cheese or dairy-free alternative (optional)

- 2 tablespoons balsamic glaze

- 2 tablespoons extra-virgin olive oil

- Salt and black pepper to taste

Instructions

- Cook the beets until tender, peel, and slice them into thin rounds.

- Peel the oranges and carefully segment them.

- In a serving platter, arrange the beet slices, orange segments, thinly sliced red onion, and torn mint leaves.

- If using, sprinkle crumbled goat cheese or dairy-free alternative over the salad.

- In a small bowl, whisk together balsamic glaze, extra-virgin olive oil, salt, and black pepper.

- Drizzle the balsamic glaze dressing over the Beet and Orange Salad.

- Serve the salad immediately, allowing the flavors to meld.

Estimated Nutritional Value (per serving)

Calories: 180, Protein: 4g, Fat: 8g, Carbohydrates: 25g, Fiber: 6g, Sugar: 18g

Tips

Use roasted or steamed beets for convenience.

Adjust the sweetness by choosing sweet or tangy oranges.

Customize with your favorite herbs like basil or parsley.

Watermelon and Mint Salad

 Prep Time: 15 minutes   Cook Time: 0 minutes

Ingredients

- 4 cups seedless watermelon, diced

- 1/2 cup fresh mint leaves, chopped

- 1/4 cup red onion, finely sliced

- 1 tablespoon lime juice

- 1 tablespoon extra-virgin olive oil

- 1/4 teaspoon salt

- 1/4 teaspoon black pepper

- 1/2 cup crumbled feta cheese (optional, omit for

  dairy-free version)

Instructions

I. Dice the seedless watermelon into bite-sized cubes.

II. In a large bowl, combine the diced watermelon, chopped fresh mint leaves, and finely sliced red onion.

III. In a small bowl, whisk together lime juice, extra-virgin olive oil, salt, and black pepper.

IV. Drizzle the lime and olive oil dressing over the watermelon mixture. Toss gently to coat.

V. If using, sprinkle crumbled feta cheese over the Watermelon and Mint Salad.

VI. Serve the salad immediately, allowing the refreshing flavors to shine.

Estimated Nutritional Value (per serving)

Calories: 80, Protein: 1g, Fat: 4g, Carbohydrates: 11g, Fiber: 1g, Sugar: 8g

Tips

Choose ripe and juicy watermelon for the best flavor.

Customize with additional herbs like basil or cilantro.

Omit the feta cheese or use a dairy-free alternative for a vegan version.

Green Bean Almondine

 Prep Time: 15 minutes   **Cook Time: 10 minutes**

Ingredients

- 1 pound green beans, ends trimmed

- 2 tablespoons olive oil

- 1/3 cup sliced almonds

- 2 cloves garlic, minced

- 1 tablespoon lemon juice

- Salt and black pepper to taste

- Lemon wedges for serving

Instructions

I.   Bring a large pot of salted water to a boil. Add the

     green beans and cook for 3-4 minutes until they

are bright green and slightly tender. Drain and transfer to an ice bath to stop the cooking process. Drain again.

II.   In a large skillet, heat olive oil over medium heat. Add sliced almonds and sauté until they are golden brown and fragrant.

III. Add Garlic and Green Beans:

IV. Add minced garlic to the skillet and sauté for about 30 seconds. Add the blanched green beans and toss to coat in the almond and garlic mixture.

V.   Drizzle lemon juice over the green beans and continue to toss until they are heated through. Season with salt and black pepper to taste.

VI. Transfer the Green Bean Almondine to a serving dish and garnish with additional sliced almonds if desired. Serve with lemon wedges on the side.

Estimated Nutritional Value (per serving)

Calories: 120, Protein: 3g, Fat: 9g, Carbohydrates: 9g, Fiber: 4g, Sugar: 3g

Tips

Choose fresh and tender green beans for the best texture.

Adjust the cooking time based on the thickness of the green beans.

Experiment with other nuts like pine nuts or walnuts for variation.

Carrot and Raisin Coleslaw

 Prep Time: 15 minutes   Cook Time: 0 minutes

Ingredients

- 4 cups shredded cabbage (green or purple)

- 1 cup shredded carrots

- 1/2 cup raisins

- 1/4 cup chopped fresh parsley

- 1/2 cup mayonnaise (dairy-free if needed)

- 2 tablespoons apple cider vinegar

- 1 tablespoon maple syrup or honey

- Salt and black pepper to taste

Instructions

I.   In a large bowl, combine shredded cabbage, shredded carrots, raisins, and chopped fresh parsley.

II. In a small bowl, whisk together mayonnaise, apple cider vinegar, maple syrup or honey, salt, and black pepper to create the dressing.

III. Pour the dressing over the cabbage and carrot mixture. Toss until the vegetables are evenly coated with the dressing.

IV. Refrigerate the Carrot and Raisin Coleslaw for at least 30 minutes before serving to allow the flavors to meld. Serve chilled.

Estimated Nutritional Value (per serving)

Calories: 150, Protein: 1g, Fat: 10g, Carbohydrates: 16g, Fiber: 2g, Sugar: 11g

Tips

Add chopped nuts, such as pecans or almonds, for extra crunch.

Experiment with different types of cabbage for a colorful coleslaw.

Adjust the sweetness of the dressing to suit your taste preferences.

Roasted Cauliflower with Turmeric

 Prep Time: 15 minutes   Roasting Time: 25 minutes

Ingredients

- 1 large head cauliflower, cut into florets

- 2 tablespoons olive oil

- 1 teaspoon ground turmeric

- 1 teaspoon ground cumin

- 1/2 teaspoon smoked paprika

- Salt and black pepper to taste

- Fresh cilantro for garnish (optional)

- Lemon wedges for serving

Instructions

I. Preheat the oven to 425°F (220°C) and line a baking sheet with parchment paper.

II. In a large bowl, toss cauliflower florets with olive oil, ground turmeric, ground cumin, smoked paprika, salt, and black pepper.

III. Spread the seasoned cauliflower on the prepared baking sheet in a single layer.

IV. Roast Until Golden:

V. Roast in the preheated oven for 25 minutes or until the cauliflower is golden brown and crisp on the edges. Toss halfway through for even roasting.

VI. Optional: Garnish the Roasted Cauliflower with fresh cilantro before serving. Serve with lemon wedges on the side.

Estimated Nutritional Value (per serving)

Calories: 100, Protein: 4g, Fat: 7g, Carbohydrates: 8g, Fiber: 4g, Sugar: 3g

Tips

Ensure even roasting by arranging cauliflower in a single layer.

Experiment with additional spices like garlic powder or chili powder.

Customize with a squeeze of fresh lemon juice before serving.

Broccoli and Apple Salad

 Prep Time: 15 minutes   Cook Time: 0 minutes

Ingredients

- 4 cups broccoli florets, blanched or steamed

- 1 large apple, cored and diced

- 1/2 cup red onion, finely chopped

- 1/2 cup dried cranberries

- 1/4 cup sunflower seeds

- 1/2 cup dairy-free mayonnaise

- 2 tablespoons apple cider vinegar

- 1 tablespoon maple syrup or honey

- Salt and black pepper to taste

Instructions

I. Blanch or steam broccoli florets until they are crisp-tender. Immediately transfer to an ice bath to retain their vibrant green color. Drain.

II. In a large bowl, combine blanched broccoli florets, diced apple, finely chopped red onion, dried cranberries, and sunflower seeds.

III. In a small bowl, whisk together dairy-free mayonnaise, apple cider vinegar, maple syrup or honey, salt, and black pepper to create the dressing.

IV. Pour the dressing over the broccoli mixture. Toss until all ingredients are well coated.

V. Refrigerate the Broccoli and Apple Salad for at least 30 minutes before serving to allow the flavors to meld. Serve chilled.

Estimated Nutritional Value (per serving)

Calories: 200, Protein: 3g, Fat: 12g, Carbohydrates: 24g, Fiber: 5g, Sugar: 15g

Tips

Customize with your favorite nuts or seeds.

Use a sweet and crisp apple variety for a refreshing flavor.

Adjust the sweetness of the dressing to suit your taste preferences.

Spinach Strawberry Salad

 Prep Time: 15 minutes   **Cook Time: 0 minutes**

Ingredients

- 6 cups fresh baby spinach

- 1 pint strawberries, hulled and sliced

- 1/2 cup sliced almonds

- 1/4 cup crumbled dairy-free feta cheese (optional)

- 1/4 cup balsamic vinaigrette dressing (store-bought or homemade)

Instructions

I.   In a large salad bowl, combine fresh baby spinach and sliced strawberries.

II.   Sprinkle sliced almonds and crumbled dairy-free feta cheese over the spinach and strawberries.

III.   Drizzle balsamic vinaigrette dressing over the salad.

IV.   Gently toss the Spinach Strawberry Salad until all ingredients are well combined. Serve immediately.

Estimated Nutritional Value (per serving)

Calories: 150, Protein: 4g, Fat: 10g, Carbohydrates: 14g, Fiber: 5g, Sugar: 7g

Tips

Add a handful of fresh mint leaves for extra freshness.

Customize with other berries like blueberries or raspberries.

Adjust the sweetness of the dressing to your taste preference.

Lemon Garlic Roasted Potatoes

 Prep Time: 15 minutes   Roasting Time: 30-35 minutes

Ingredients

- 2 pounds baby potatoes, halved

- 3 tablespoons olive oil

- 3 cloves garlic, minced

- 1 teaspoon dried rosemary

- 1 teaspoon dried thyme

- Zest of 1 lemon

- Salt and black pepper to taste

- Fresh parsley for garnish (optional)

Instructions

I. Preheat the oven to 400°F (200°C) and line a baking sheet with parchment paper.

II. In a large bowl, toss halved baby potatoes with olive oil, minced garlic, dried rosemary, dried thyme, lemon zest, salt, and black pepper.

III. Spread the seasoned potatoes on the prepared baking sheet in a single layer.

IV. Roast in the preheated oven for 30-35 minutes or until the potatoes are golden brown and crispy on the edges. Toss halfway through for even cooking.

V. Optional: Garnish the Lemon Garlic Roasted Potatoes with fresh parsley before serving.

Estimated Nutritional Value (per serving)

Calories: 180, Protein: 3g, Fat: 8g, Carbohydrates: 25g, Fiber: 3g, Sugar: 2g

Tips

Use a mix of baby potatoes for variety in color and texture.

Experiment with additional herbs like parsley or chives.

Squeeze fresh lemon juice over the potatoes before serving for extra zing.

CHAPTER FIVE

Desserts

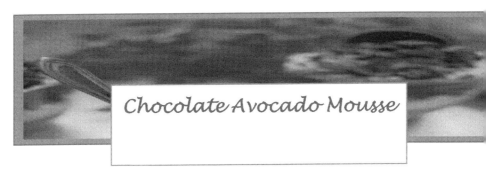

Chocolate Avocado Mousse

 Prep Time: 10 minutes   Chilling Time: 2 Hours

Ingredients

- 2 ripe avocados, peeled and pitted

- 1/2 cup unsweetened cocoa powder

- 1/2 cup maple syrup or agave nectar

- 1 teaspoon vanilla extract

- A pinch of salt

- Fresh berries for garnish (optional)

Instructions

- In a food processor or blender, combine ripe avocados, cocoa powder, maple syrup or agave nectar, vanilla extract, and a pinch of salt.

- Blend the ingredients until smooth and creamy. Scrape down the sides as needed to ensure even blending.

- Transfer the chocolate avocado mixture to serving bowls or glasses. Chill in the refrigerator for at least 2 hours to allow the mousse to set.

- Optional: Garnish with fresh berries before serving.

Estimated Nutritional Value (per serving)

Calories: 200, Protein: 3g, Fat: 12g, Carbohydrates: 25g, Fiber: 8g, Sugar: 14g

Tips

Use ripe avocados for a smoother texture and natural sweetness.

Adjust the sweetness by adding more or less maple syrup or agave nectar.

Experiment with flavored extracts like peppermint or almond for variation.

Chocolate Avocado Mousse

 Prep Time: 10 minutes   **Chilling Time: 2 Hours**

Ingredients

- 3 ripe bananas, mashed

- 1/4 cup coconut oil, melted

- 1/4 cup maple syrup or honey

- 1 teaspoon vanilla extract

- 1/2 cup coconut flour

- 1 teaspoon baking soda

- 1/2 teaspoon cinnamon

- A pinch of salt

- Chopped nuts or shredded coconut for topping (optional)

Instructions

I.   Preheat the oven to 350°F (175°C). Grease a loaf pan or line it with parchment paper.

II. In a large bowl, whisk together mashed bananas,, melted coconut oil, maple syrup or honey, and vanilla extract.

III. In a separate bowl, combine coconut flour, baking soda, cinnamon, and a pinch of salt.

IV. Add the dry ingredients to the wet ingredients and mix until well combined. Let the batter sit for a few minutes to allow the coconut flour to absorb the liquid.

V.   Pour the batter into the prepared loaf pan, spreading it evenly. Optional: Top with chopped nuts or shredded coconut.

VI.   Bake in the preheated oven for 45-50 minutes or until a toothpick inserted into the center comes out clean.

VII.   Allow the Coconut Flour Banana Bread to cool in the pan for 10 minutes before transferring it to a wire rack to cool completely. Slice and serve.

Estimated Nutritional Value (per serving)

Calories: 180, Protein: 4g, Fat: 10g, Carbohydrates: 20g, Fiber: 4g, Sugar: 11g

Tips

Use very ripe bananas for natural sweetness and flavor.

Adjust sweetness by adding more or less maple syrup or honey.

Customize with add-ins like chocolate chips or dried fruit for variety.

Berry Sorbet

 Prep Time: 10 minutes   Freezing Time: 4-6 Hours

Ingredients

- 3 cups mixed berries (strawberries, blueberries, raspberries)
- 1/4 cup maple syrup or agave nectar
- 1 tablespoon fresh lemon juice
- 1/2 cup water

Instructions

I. In a blender, combine mixed berries, maple syrup or agave nectar, fresh lemon juice, and water.

II. Blend the ingredients until smooth and well combined.

III.   Optional: Strain the mixture through a fine-mesh sieve to remove seeds and pulp for a smoother sorbet.

IV.   Transfer the sorbet mixture to a shallow dish or ice cream maker. Freeze for 4-6 hours, stirring or churning every hour to prevent ice crystals.

V.   Scoop the Berry Sorbet into bowls or cones. Garnish with fresh berries if desired.

Estimated Nutritional Value (per serving)

Calories: 80, Protein: 1g, Fat: 0g, Carbohydrates: 20g, Fiber: 4g, Sugar: 14g

Tips

Experiment with different berry combinations for variety.

Adjust sweetness by adding more or less maple syrup or agave nectar.

Customize with a splash of your favorite fruit juice for extra flavor.

Pumpkin Pie Chia Pudding

 Prep Time: 10 minutes   Chilling Time: 4-6 Hours

Ingredients

- 1/2 cup canned pumpkin puree

- 2 cups unsweetened almond milk or any plant-based milk

- 1/4 cup chia seeds

- 2 tablespoons maple syrup or agave nectar

- 1 teaspoon pumpkin pie spice

- 1 teaspoon vanilla extract

- Pecans or whipped coconut cream for garnish (optional)

Instructions

I.   In a bowl, whisk together canned pumpkin puree, almond milk, chia seeds, maple syrup or agave nectar, pumpkin pie spice, and vanilla extract.

II. Whisk the ingredients until well combined. Ensure there are no lumps.

III. Cover the bowl and refrigerate the Pumpkin Pie Chia Pudding for at least 4 hours or overnight to allow the chia seeds to absorb the liquid and thicken.

IV. Before serving, give the pudding a good stir to evenly distribute the chia seeds. If it's too thick, you can add a bit more almond milk.

V.   Optional: Garnish with pecans or a dollop of whipped coconut cream before serving.

Estimated Nutritional Value (per serving)

Calories: 180, Protein: 4g, Fat: 8g, Carbohydrates: 25g, Fiber: 8g, Sugar: 12g

Tips

Adjust sweetness and spice levels to suit your taste.

Experiment with different plant-based milk options.

Customize with a sprinkle of cinnamon or nutmeg for extra flavor.

Apple Cinnamon Oat Cookies

 Prep Time: 15 minutes   Baking Time: 12-15 Minutes

Ingredients

- 2 cups old-fashioned oats (certified gluten-free if needed)

- 1 cup grated apple (about 1 medium-sized apple)

- 1/2 cup coconut oil, melted

- 1/4 cup maple syrup or agave nectar

- 1 teaspoon ground cinnamon

- 1/2 teaspoon baking soda

- 1/4 teaspoon salt

- 1/2 cup raisins or chopped dried apples (optional)

Instructions

I. Preheat the oven to 350°F (175°C). Line a baking sheet with parchment paper.

II. In a large bowl, combine old-fashioned oats, grated apple, melted coconut oil, maple syrup or agave nectar, ground cinnamon, baking soda, and salt. Mix until well combined.

III. If using, fold in raisins or chopped dried apples into the cookie dough.

IV. Using a cookie scoop or spoon, drop rounded portions of the dough onto the prepared baking sheet. Flatten each cookie slightly with the back of the spoon.

V. Bake in the preheated oven for 12-15 minutes or until the edges are golden brown.

VI. Allow the Apple Cinnamon Oat Cookies to cool on the baking sheet for a few minutes before transferring them to a wire rack to cool completely.

Estimated Nutritional Value (per serving)

Calories: 120, Protein: 2g, Fat: 7g, Carbohydrates: 14g, Fiber: 2g, Sugar: 6g

Tips

Choose a sweet apple variety for natural sweetness.

Customize with nuts or seeds for added crunch.

Store in an airtight container for freshness.

Mango Sorbet with Lime

 Prep Time: 10 minutes   **Freezing Time: 4-6 Hours**

Ingredients

- 4 cups ripe mango chunks (fresh or frozen)

- 1/4 cup maple syrup or agave nectar

- Juice of 2 limes

- 1/2 cup water

Instructions

I.   In a blender, combine ripe mango chunks, maple syrup or agave nectar, lime juice, and water.

II.   Blend the ingredients until smooth and well combined.

III. Optional: Strain the mixture through a fine-mesh sieve to remove any fibers for a smoother sorbet.

IV. Transfer the sorbet mixture to a shallow dish or ice cream maker. Freeze for 4-6 hours, stirring or churning every hour to prevent ice crystals.

V. Scoop the Mango Sorbet into bowls or cones. Garnish with lime zest or mint leaves if desired.

Estimated Nutritional Value (per serving)

Calories: 100, Protein: 1g, Fat: 0g, Carbohydrates: 25g, Fiber: 2g, Sugar: 22g

Tips

Use ripe and sweet mangoes for the best flavor.

Adjust sweetness by adding more or less maple syrup or agave nectar.

Experiment with adding a pinch of chili powder for a hint of heat.

Almond Joy Energy Bites

 Prep Time: 15 minutes Chilling Time: 30 Minutes

Ingredients

- 1 cup rolled oats (certified gluten-free if needed)

- 1/2 cup almond butter

- 1/4 cup maple syrup or agave nectar

- 1/4 cup shredded coconut (plus extra for coating)

- 1/4 cup chopped almonds

- 2 tablespoons cocoa powder

- 1 teaspoon vanilla extract

- A pinch of salt

Instructions

I. In a large bowl, combine rolled oats, almond butter, maple syrup or agave nectar, shredded coconut, chopped almonds, cocoa powder, vanilla extract, and a pinch of salt.

II. Stir the ingredients until well combined. If the mixture is too sticky, you can add more rolled oats.

III. Chill:

IV. Place the mixture in the refrigerator for at least 30 minutes to firm up.

V. Form Energy Bites:

VI. Take small portions of the chilled mixture and roll them into bite-sized balls.

VII. Optional: Roll the Almond Joy Energy Bites in shredded coconut for an extra layer of flavor.

VIII. For a firmer texture, chill the energy bites again before serving.

Estimated Nutritional Value (per serving)

Calories: 120, Protein: 3g, Fat: 8g, Carbohydrates: 10g, Fiber: 2g, Sugar: 4g

Tips

Customize with your favorite nuts or seeds.

Adjust sweetness by adding more or less maple syrup or agave nectar.

Store in an airtight container in the refrigerator for freshness.

Lemon Poppy Seed Muffins Baked Cinnamon Apples

Baked Cinnamon Apples

 Prep Time: 10 minutes   **Baking Time: 25-30 Minutes**

Ingredients

- 4 large apples, cored and sliced

- 2 tablespoons coconut oil, melted

- 2 tablespoons maple syrup or agave nectar

- 1 teaspoon ground cinnamon

- 1/4 teaspoon nutmeg

- A pinch of salt

- Chopped nuts for garnish (optional)

Instructions

I.   Preheat the oven to 375°F (190°C). Grease a baking dish.

II.   In a large bowl, toss sliced apples with melted coconut oil, maple syrup or agave nectar, ground cinnamon, nutmeg, and a pinch of salt.

III. Arrange the coated apple slices in a single layer in the prepared baking dish.

IV.   Bake in the preheated oven for 25-30 minutes or until the apples are tender, stirring halfway through.

V.   Optional: Garnish the Baked Cinnamon Apples with chopped nuts before serving.

Estimated Nutritional Value (per serving)

Calories: 150, Protein: 1g, Fat: 6g, Carbohydrates: 25g, Fiber: 5g, Sugar: 18g

Tips

Choose sweet apple varieties like Honeycrisp or Gala.

Customize with a sprinkle of granola or shredded coconut.

Adjust sweetness and spice levels to suit your taste.

CHAPTER SIX

Beverages

Green Detox Smoothie

Prep Time: 10 minutes

Ingredients

- 1 cup spinach leaves

- 1/2 cucumber, peeled and sliced

- 1/2 green apple, cored and chopped

- 1/2 lemon, juiced

- 1/2 inch fresh ginger, peeled

- 1 cup coconut water

- 1/2 cup ice cubes

- Optional: 1 tablespoon chia seeds or flaxseeds

Instructions

I. In a blender, combine spinach leaves, cucumber slices, green apple chunks, lemon juice, fresh ginger, coconut water, and ice cubes.

II. Blend the ingredients until smooth and creamy.

III. Optional: Add chia seeds or flaxseeds and blend for a nutrient boost.

IV. Pour the Green Detox Smoothie into a glass and enjoy immediately.

Estimated Nutritional Value (per serving)

Calories: 80, Protein: 2g, Fat: 0g, Carbohydrates: 20g, Fiber: 5g, Sugar: 10g

Tips

Use frozen green apple chunks for a chilled smoothie.

Adjust sweetness by adding more or less apple or a touch of maple syrup.

Experiment with other greens like kale or arugula for variety.

Turmeric Golden Milk Latte

Ingredients

- 1 cup unsweetened almond milk or coconut milk

- 1 teaspoon ground turmeric

- 1/2 teaspoon ground cinnamon

- 1/4 teaspoon ground ginger

- 1 tablespoon maple syrup or agave nectar (adjust to taste)

- 1/2 teaspoon vanilla extract

- A pinch of black pepper (increases turmeric absorption)

- Optional: Dash of ground cardamom

Instructions

I.   In a small saucepan, heat almond milk or coconut milk over medium heat until warmed but not boiling.

II. Whisk in ground turmeric, ground cinnamon, ground ginger, maple syrup or agave nectar, vanilla extract, and a pinch of black pepper.

III. Simmer the mixture for 2-3 minutes, allowing the flavors to meld. Do not boil.

IV. Optional: Strain the Turmeric Golden Milk through a fine-mesh sieve to remove any residue.

V.   Pour the Turmeric Golden Milk Latte into a mug and enjoy the comforting warmth.

Estimated Nutritional Value (per serving)

Calories: 60, Protein: 1g, Fat: 3g, Carbohydrates: 10g, Fiber: 1g, Sugar: 7g

Tips

Adjust sweetness and spice levels to suit your taste.

Use fresh turmeric if available for a vibrant color and added freshness.

Experiment with other plant-based milk alternatives like oat or soy milk.

Berry Mint Sparkling Water

Prep Time: 5 minutes

Ingredients

- 1 cup mixed berries (strawberries, blueberries, raspberries)
- 1/4 cup fresh mint leaves
- 1 tablespoon agave nectar or maple syrup
- 1 lemon, sliced
- 4 cups sparkling water
- Ice cubes

Instructions

I. In a pitcher, muddle the mixed berries and fresh mint leaves to release their flavors.

II. Add agave nectar or maple syrup to the muddled berries and mint. Stir to combine.

III. Add sliced lemon to the pitcher for a citrusy twist.

IV. Pour sparkling water into the pitcher, over the muddled berries, mint, and lemon.

V. Gently stir the Berry Mint Sparkling Water to combine all the ingredients.

VI. Pour the sparkling water over ice into glasses. Garnish with additional mint leaves and berries if desired.

Estimated Nutritional Value (per serving)

Calories: 20, Protein: 0g, Fat: 0g, Carbohydrates: 5g, Fiber: 1g, Sugar: 3g

Tips

Adjust sweetness by adding more or less agave nectar or maple syrup.

Experiment with different herb combinations like basil or thyme.

Make a large batch and keep it chilled for a quick and healthy beverage.

Cucumber Lemonade

Prep Time: 10 minutes   **Chilling Time: 1-2 hours**

Ingredients

- 2 cucumbers, peeled and sliced

- 1 cup fresh lemon juice (about 4-6 lemons)

- 1/2 cup agave nectar or honey

- 6 cups water

- Ice cubes

- Lemon slices and cucumber ribbons for garnish

Instructions

I. In a blender, blend the sliced cucumbers until smooth. Strain the cucumber puree to extract the juice.

II. In a large pitcher, combine the cucumber juice, fresh lemon juice, agave nectar or honey, and water. Stir well.

III. Refrigerate the Cucumber Lemonade for 1-2 hours to allow the flavors to meld.

IV. Before serving, add ice cubes to glasses and pour the chilled Cucumber Lemonade over the ice.

V. Garnish with lemon slices and cucumber ribbons for a decorative touch.

Estimated Nutritional Value (per serving)

Calories: 80, Protein: 1g, Fat: 0g, Carbohydrates: 20g, Fiber: 1g, Sugar: 15g

Tips

Adjust sweetness by adding more or less agave nectar or honey.

Experiment with adding a handful of fresh mint leaves for extra freshness.

Make a batch and keep it chilled for a cool and revitalizing drink.

Hibiscus Iced Tea

Prep Time: 5 minutes   Steeping   and   Chilling

Time: 2-3 hours

Ingredients

- 4 hibiscus tea bags

- 4 cups hot water

- 1/4 cup agave nectar or honey (adjust to taste)

- 1 orange, sliced

- Ice cubes

- Fresh mint leaves for garnish

Instructions

I. Place hibiscus tea bags in a heatproof pitcher. Pour hot water over the tea bags and steep for 5-7 minutes.

II. Remove the tea bags and add agave nectar or honey to the steeped hibiscus tea. Stir until the sweetener dissolves.

III. Add sliced orange to the hibiscus tea for a citrusy flavor.

IV. Allow the Hibiscus Iced Tea to cool to room temperature, then refrigerate for 2-3 hours or until thoroughly chilled.

V. Fill glasses with ice cubes and pour the chilled Hibiscus Iced Tea over the ice.

VI. Garnish with fresh mint leaves for a refreshing touch.

Estimated Nutritional Value (per serving)

Calories: 30, Protein: 0g, Fat: 0g, Carbohydrates: 8g, Fiber: 0g, Sugar: 7g

Tips

Adjust sweetness by adding more or less agave nectar or honey.

Experiment with adding a cinnamon stick or ginger for additional flavor.

Make a large batch for a refreshing and hydrating drink throughout the day.

Cranberry Orange Mocktail

Prep Time: 5 minutes

Ingredients

- 1 cup cranberry juice (unsweetened)

- 1/2 cup orange juice (freshly squeezed)

- 1 tablespoon agave nectar or maple syrup

- Sparkling water

- Ice cubes

- Orange slices and fresh cranberries for garnish

Instructions

I. In a glass, combine cranberry juice, freshly squeezed orange juice, and agave nectar or maple syrup. Stir well.

II. Top the juice mixture with sparkling water to your desired level of fizziness.

III. Gently stir the Cranberry Orange Mocktail to combine the flavors.

IV. Add ice cubes to the glass for a refreshing chill.

V. Garnish with orange slices and fresh cranberries for a festive touch.

Estimated Nutritional Value (per serving)

Calories: 60, Protein: 0g, Fat: 0g, Carbohydrates: 15g, Fiber: 1g, Sugar: 12g

Tips

Adjust sweetness by adding more or less agave nectar or maple syrup.

Experiment with different fruit garnishes like lime wedges or berries.

Rim the glass with sugar for an added touch of sweetness.

Ginger Turmeric Lemonade

Prep Time: 10 minutes   **Chilling Time: 1-2 hours**

Ingredients

- 4 cups water

- 1/2 cup fresh lemon juice (about 3-4 lemons)

- 1/4 cup agave nectar or honey

- 1 tablespoon fresh ginger, grated

- 1 teaspoon ground turmeric

- Ice cubes

- Lemon slices and fresh mint leaves for garnish

Instructions

I. In a pitcher, combine water, fresh lemon juice, agave nectar or honey, grated fresh ginger, and ground turmeric. Stir well.

II. Refrigerate the Ginger Turmeric Lemonade for 1-2 hours to allow the flavors to meld.

III. Optional: Strain the lemonade through a fine-mesh sieve to remove ginger and turmeric particles.

IV. Fill glasses with ice cubes and pour the chilled Ginger Turmeric Lemonade over the ice.

V. Garnish with lemon slices and fresh mint leaves for a decorative touch.

Estimated Nutritional Value (per serving)

Calories: 50, Protein: 0g, Fat: 0g, Carbohydrates: 15g, Fiber: 0g, Sugar: 10g

Tips

Adjust sweetness by adding more or less agave nectar or honey.

Experiment with adding a pinch of black pepper for enhanced turmeric absorption.

Make a large batch and keep it chilled for a cool and revitalizing drink.

Peach and Mint Iced Tea

Prep Time: 15 minutes   Steeping and Chilling Time: 2-3 hours

Ingredients

- 4 ripe peaches, sliced
- 1/4 cup fresh mint leaves
- 4 black tea bags
- 4 cups hot water
- 1/4 cup agave nectar or honey (adjust to taste)

- Ice cubes

- Peach slices and mint sprigs for garnish

Instructions

I.   In a heatproof pitcher, combine sliced peaches and fresh mint leaves.

II. Place black tea bags in the pitcher with the peaches and mint. Pour hot water over the tea bags and steep for 5-7 minutes.

III. Remove the tea bags and add agave nectar or honey to the peach and mint-infused tea. Stir until the sweetener dissolves.

IV. Allow the Peach and Mint Iced Tea to cool to room temperature, then refrigerate for 2-3 hours or until thoroughly chilled.

V.   Fill glasses with ice cubes and pour the chilled Peach and Mint Iced Tea over the ice.

VI.   Garnish with peach slices and mint sprigs for a delightful presentation.

Estimated Nutritional Value (per serving)

Calories: 40, Protein: 0g, Fat: 0g, Carbohydrates: 10g, Fiber: 1g, Sugar: 9g

Tips

Adjust sweetness by adding more or less agave nectar or honey.

Experiment with different tea blends like green tea or herbal tea.

Include a squeeze of fresh lemon or lime juice for a citrusy twist.

Raspberry Lime Sparkler

Prep Time: 10 minutes   Chilling Time: 1 hour (optional)

Ingredients

- 1 cup fresh raspberries

- 2 limes, juiced

- 1/4 cup agave nectar or honey (adjust to taste)

- 3 cups sparkling water

- Ice cubes

- Lime slices and fresh raspberries for garnish

Instructions

I.   In a blender, combine fresh raspberries, lime juice, and agave nectar or honey. Blend until smooth.

II. Optional: Strain the raspberry-lime mixture through a fine-mesh sieve to remove seeds and pulp.

III. Refrigerate the Raspberry Lime mixture for 1 hour for a chilled sparkler.

IV. Fill glasses with ice cubes. Pour the chilled or room temperature Raspberry Lime mixture into each glass.

V.   Top each glass with sparkling water for a fizzy and refreshing sparkler.

VI.   Gently stir the Raspberry Lime Sparkler to combine the flavors.

VII.   Garnish with lime slices and fresh raspberries for a delightful presentation.

Estimated Nutritional Value (per serving)

Calories: 50, Protein: 1g, Fat: 0g, Carbohydrates: 12g, Fiber: 3g, Sugar: 8g

Tips

Adjust sweetness by adding more or less agave nectar or honey.

Experiment with different berries like blackberries or strawberries.

Make a large batch and keep it chilled for a quick and healthy beverage.

Made in the USA
Monee, IL
11 March 2025

13864467R00142